BIBLIO1

AIRBUS vs BOEING

Conforti, Facundo Jorge
   Airbus vs Boeing / Facundo Jorge Conforti. - 1a ed . - Mar del Plata : Facundo Jorge Conforti, 2020.
   200 p. ; 21 x 14 cm. - (How does it work? ; 27)

   1. Aviación. 2. Aviación Civil. 3. Aeronáutica. I. Título.
   CDD 629.133

Fecha de Catalogación: 07/25/2022

Facundo Conforti, 2022.

Translated by Mariana G. Gallo (Aeronautical Library's official translator)

Published in Argentina. This handbook is sold subject to the condition that it shall not, by way of trade or otherwise, be lent, re-sold, hired out, or otherwise circulated without the publisher's prior consent.

Preface

The aeronautical industry has been captivated by different engineering works over the decades. In more than 100 years of aviation, humanity has enjoyed countless achievements on the part of the aeronautical pioneers who marked a point in the history of transport. In the face of a constantly growing aeronautical market, new entrepreneurs and dreamers have been encouraged to develop their own aircraft with which, in some cases, they have managed to enter the aeronautical world.

But all this has a starting point where everything begins with a vision. This beginning has not been alien to the two major companies in the aeronautical industry, Airbus and Boeing. Two giants of the aeronautical world that transcended borders and overcame the most insurmountable challenges that man had set himself in the aeronautical sector within its short life. Throughout the pages, we will learn about the beginnings of these two giants starting with the history of each one and analyzing their evolution over time. Two industry leaders who continue to offer majestic engineering works in the service of commercial and military aviation.

The undisputed leaders of the aeronautical industry are detailed from their commencement to the present times where they continue to innovate with state-of-the-art aircraft that overrun the market.

Main

Chapter 1 – BOEING

The Boeing history   07

Chapter 2 – AIRBUS

The Boeing History   61

Chapter 3 – Presidential Aircrafts

Introduction	103
United State presidential aircraft	106
France presidential aircraft	115
México presidential aircraft	118
Germany presidential aircraft	120
Japan presidential aircraft	124

Chapter 4 – Titans fight. A320 vs B737

Introduction	127
Airbus A320 family	130
Boeing B737 models	134
Titans fight	139

Chapter 5 – Executive Aircrafts

Introduction   151
Boeing Executive Line   154
Airbus Executive Line   165

Chapter 6 – Giants fight. B747 vs A380

Introduction   177
B747 models   180
A380 models   183
Giants fight   188

Chapter 2

The History of BOEING

The History of Boeing

Boeing Company is one of the largest airlines in the world along with its main competitor Airbus. Two empires of world aviation. Let's know the beginning of the Boeing empire.

It all starts with Mr. William Boeing, a man dedicated to the family business of forestry and mining. The family had settled in Minnesota when they arrived from Germany in search of the American dream. Wilhelm Böing (Boeing comes from "Americanizing" the surname) had managed to establish a small fortune thanks to wood and iron mines. Sadly, William's father died of the flu when he was only 8 years old. By then, the family business was constantly growing. Little William was able to go to study in Switzerland and enrol in Yale University on the way back (although he did not graduate, he dropped out in the last year).

After leaving college William Boeing embarked on creating his own logging company in Washington state. William's good sense of smell for business coupled with family experience in the sector made Boeing manage to amass large amounts of money in a few years. Moved by the growth of the company, William decides to move the headquarters of his company to Seattle.

Unknowingly, that decision would turn Seattle into one of the aviation capitals of the world years later.

The year 1909 had arrived and the young Boeing approached a new trade fair that had been preparing for some time in the state capital, the "Alaska Yukon Pacific Expo". Three million people would pass through the premises of a fair that promoted an airship flight by a pioneer named James Mars. That exhibition along with the demonstration of that flight, would forever mark William Boeing.

Fascinated by his first encounter with those flying wonders of the time, William continued to attend all the thematic exhibitions of the country and that was how he arrived at the renowned expo of the time known as "Los Angeles Air Meet" where the attendees were exposed amazing flights and world records. This exhibition was a great international event where exhibitors from all over the world presented their models of flying machines, making demonstration flights in order to gain prestige over the few creations that existed in the market. The event was held in the open field with grandstands from where people could enjoy the novel spectacle of seeing a man-made machine fly.

In some biographies it is said that Boeing was looking among the pilots for someone who would give him a flight in these new machines, but he only received refusals from those pioneers of aviation. In fact, William would spend the next five years of his life looking for someone to help him experience the sensation of flying, but again and again he received refusals from the few pilots of the time and almost always with the same answer: getting on those models of experimental flying machines was very dangerous and, on many occasions, they ended up accidented.

On one of his many trips to exhibitions and air festivals he met George Westervelt, a naval engineer who worked for the US Navy. They quickly forged a friendship that shared a common theme: aviation. Westervelt worked as an engineer in the design and maintenance of U.S. Navy seaplanes. Their friendship continued to grow steadily thanks to William's passion for aviation and George's dedication to his work on navy seaplanes. Years later they would go further doing aeronautical business together.

Arriving in 1914, William Boeing achieves his goal, a pioneer of aviation based in Los Angeles named Terah Maroney flies to Seattle with the aim of giving Boeing the opportunity to know the flight. William, without hesitation, planned his trip to Los Angeles to fulfil his goal and try to go further and obtain the flight lessons necessary to become a pilot. Fortunately, he had enough financial backing for such an adventure.

Arriving in Los Angeles, he goes directly to one of the few academies that existed at that time, a place directed by Glenn L. Martin (Founder of the current Lockheed Martin company). Martin was one of the most prestigious aviation pioneers of that era. Famous for designing and building his own aircraft made with bamboo reeds, wood and fabric. Considering his finantial possibilities, William decides to buy a model of his planes from Glenn Martin on the condition that he himself teach him to fly in the machine he had bought.

Already consecrated as an enthusiastic pilot, William continued to fly his own seaplane known as "Flying Birdcare" until in an unfortunate accident his flying machine broke down because of the blow. Glenn Martin informed William that there would be no spare parts available to change the broken parts on his plane for a couple of months. It was at that time that William considered that at that time he could build his own aircraft and start his aeronautical business.

Back in Seattle, William talks again with his old friend George Westeverlt and bringing him up to date with the situation he was going through, both decide what they could start making their own model. Convinced by the idea that the union of a pilot and wood expert (Boeing) with an expert engineer in seaplanes (Westervelt) would result in an aircraft superior to those of Martin, in January 1916 both launched the design of a new seaplane that a few months later would be baptized with the name of "Bluebill": the first "B&W Seaplane", which would later go down in history as the Boeing Model 1, a model that would be born on the shores of Lake Union, where the Boeing timber company was established.

Just before the Model 1 made its first flight on June 15, 1916 with Boeing inside, the company suffered its first unforeseen event: its partner George Westervelt was transferred to Washington by the US Navy. Already with the Model 1 tested in flight and with a view to selling several units to the American Navy thanks to the contacts of Westervelt, a month after the first flight, on July 15, 1916 the "Pacific Aero Products" was officially born, what we know today as "The Boeing Company".

Unfortunately, despite Westervelt's influences in the navy, Boeing fails to sell a single Model 1 unit to the navy. This would be the company's first commercial failure. Only two examples of the Model 1 were built and were subsequently sold to the New Zealand Postal Service.

Like every pioneer, William Boeing never gave up on failure. With his enormous financial backing and despite the recent commercial failure and the departure of his friend George Westeverlt, he decides to expand. The old shipyard that Boeing had bought 6 years earlier would be dedicated to the design and assembly of aircraft of the company, already renamed in 1917 officially as "Boeing Airplane Company".

Boeing's ambition had no limits. He had funded the wind tunnel project at the University of Washington to obtain the analyses of each study and with the plan to recruit the best engineers from the class. That's how he hired an aeronautical engineer named James Foley and a Chinese aeronautical engineer named Wong Tsu. Luck seemed to change for William when at the end of 1917 the United States enters the First World War and sees a good opportunity to sell (indeed) his seaplanes to the US Navy. To make a good impression, Boeing plans his new model with the support of his new engineers with deep knowledge of aeronautics and creates the Model C.

Already confident with the improvements of his machine, he takes it in containers to Pensacola where it would be tested by the US Navy. Boeing's new flying machine demonstrated qualities far superior to its commercial rivals. Because of the great impression left by the demonstration, U.S. Navy personnel asked William how long it would take to deliver 20 units identical to the one in the demonstration. It was the company's first major commercial success. Indeed, a few days later Boeing signed a contract for 50 seaplanes to be delivered in 1918.

When World War I ended, in 1918, there was a large surplus of used military aircraft, which were sold cheaply, flooding the market for commercial aircraft. This prevented aircraft companies, such as Boeing, from selling new aircraft. Because of this, many companies in the aviation sector abandoned the business, but other companies, including Boeing, began to sell other products. Boeing began building dressers, countertops and furniture, along with flat-bottomed ships.

The financial backing that William Boeing had generated in his years as a timber entrepreneur had given him the opportunity to pass the crisis without economic shocks, and even trying his luck with new projects. Far from abandoning its aeronautical vision, just a year later, in 1919, the company would build its new aircraft for commercial purposes, the B-1 model intended to carry correspondence from Seattle to Canada, work that the aircraft carried out successfully for eight years.

Once again, the geniuses of William Boeing had launched his company after the commercial crisis it was going through. After his new commercial success, William decides to insist with the armed forces and it was again the army that saved the company. In 1921 Boeing won the contract to build 200 aircraft with the MB-3 model, a biplane used as a fighter by the US Army of the time.

After several models behind him (the most successful in the military section), in 1927 there would be another important moment in the history of Boeing: the privatization of the United States postal service would give the company the opportunity to sell its latest model at that time, the Boeing Model 40. A biplane with a radial engine and improved performance compared to its previous versions. The 40A model was designed exclusively for the development of postal activity in the United States. Already at that time the established businessman William Boeing was part of the nation's postal air services business.

To operate his growing airmail business, William founded Boeing Air Transport (BAT) in 1927. After a series of acquisitions and mergers and the passage of the Airmail Act of 1934, BAT would give life to United Airlines.

William Boeing's wonderful entrepreneurial skills would soon lead the company to success. Boeing decides to modify the aircraft in order to offer the lowest offer in the market to the American government and wins the contract for the mail route between San Francisco and Chicago in January 1927 with an unbeatable offer: Boeing would put $ 500,000 as a guarantee and would have 26 operational aircraft by July 1 of that year. This would be the first step for the consolidated growth of the company commanded by Boeing.

William Boeing's new vision had taken flight. The company Boeing Air Transport, had incorporated the possibility of transporting passengers, in addition to the frequent postal service. During the first year of management with the new transport service, the company achieved a record of almost 1800 passengers transported. Today it seems a very small number, but considering that, at that time, the transport aircraft only carried 5 passengers per flight, thinking about a number of 1800 people transported makes us see the dimension of the success of the firm.

Quickly came the depression of 1930, a situation that would affect the interests of the company and put a pause to the constant progress of Boeing. But far from giving up and backed by a huge capital generated in recent years, the company is once again betting on the development of new products and manufacturing the first low-wing aircraft, the Boeing 200 or Monomail. A totally innovative model, more aerodynamic and agile than its previous models.

It was made entirely of metal, was fast and aerodynamic and had a retractable landing gear. In fact, its design was so novel that the engines and propellers of the time would not have been able to handle that aircraft. When controllable pitch propellers were developed, Boeing was building its Model 247 aircraft with a cabin for 6 passengers.

It was the first modern airline aircraft. A twin-engine airline car that could fly with a single engine. In an era of unreliable engines, this greatly improved flight safety. Boeing built the first seventy aircraft exclusively for the operations of its own subsidiary airline, United Airlines. The market was already consolidated by a new passenger transport industry, with new aircraft, safer and more comfortable than the first models. This gained the trust of the public that was encouraged to fly more and more. In order to continue adding comfort services to its flights, the company employs on-board staff to offer an exclusive assistance service during the journey.

With unimaginable growth, the company transported passengers and mail at the same time, which made the business extremely profitable. This hurt competing companies and the U.S. government requested that it be banned at the time. That's when in 1934, the Air Mail Act prohibited airlines and manufacturers from being under the same corporate name, so the company split into three smaller companies: Boeing Airplane Company, United Airlines, and United Aircraft Corporation. After hundreds of legal ups and downs, a U.S. senator questioned Boeing's financial credibility, questioning such a rapid growth of a company like Boeing in a sector that was recently appearing on the market.

After an investigation, Senator Black accuses Boeing of monopolistic practices: it designs aircraft for United and does not grant delivery slots to any other airline. And to top it off, the scandal called "Air Mail Fiasco" has just erupted, airlines made passenger flights on government-subsidized routes to transport mail, just what Boeing did on its first route (Chicago San Francisco). Public opinion was launched against those airlines that made subsidized flights with public money fraudulently. Due to the legal conflicts, already publicly disclosed, William Boeing decides to leave the company after more than two decades of dedication to the new aeronautical market. He would spend his time investing racehorses, buying real estate, and sailing on his yacht. But even so, he would never cease to be present in one way or another in the company. Even on the flight of the company's first jet, the Dash 80, William and his wife would be among the invited VIPs. It would be the last plane with his last name he would see fly.

On September 28, 1956, William Boeing died at the age of 65 of a heart attack. But the years ran its course and the Boeing company, already consolidated as one of the largest aircraft factories in the world, continued its progress.

After leaving the company, William had appointed his friend Claire Egtvedt, who had become president of Boeing in 1933, as a director. He had a somewhat different view of the aviation industry than William did. Claire believed that the future of the company lay in building larger aircraft. This new stage of the company would be led by a different entrepreneur. Thinking on a large scale was the goal of the new president of the Boeing firm. Undoubtedly, quite a challenge, considering the bad publicity that the company had taken with the negative statements of Senator Black, but it seemed that Claire was not afraid of challenges and had the support of his friend and founder William Boeing.

Following his vision, in 1936 he ordered the start of construction work on Boeing's second factory (Boeing Plant 2) to accommodate the production of larger aircraft. An ambitious construction that would implement an unparalleled production line, with hundreds of employees, large-scale production machinery, engineers and a whole avant-garde logistics for the time.

Soon after comes the first stroke of luck for the "New Boeing". Hand in hand with its new president and with a new business vision, an agreement was reached with the airline PANAM to develop a commercial aircraft capable of carrying passengers on transoceanic routes.

From that need comes the Boeing 314 Clipper project. It was a completely different plane from the rest. It had a capacity to accommodate 74 passengers in seven luxurious compartments and 10 crew; It also had a dining room with capacity for 14 people and a "bridal suite" in the back, near the tail of the plane, on night flights accommodated 40 passengers in bunk beds. Claire's ambitious vision was coming to light and seemed to be the right path for the company's development. The first flight of the Boeing 314 Clipper was in June 1938.

Boeing's time and successes were ongoing. World War II was looming and Claire knew that there was a market with a lot of potential and with a client already known to the firm, the armed forces of the United States. His vision was right again. Boeing manufactured a large number of bombers such as the B-17 Flying Fortress and the B-29 SuperFortress.

By early March 1944, production had increased so much that 350 aircraft were being built each month. To protect themselves from air strikes, the factories were covered with vegetation and agricultural elements.

After World War II, the need for military bombers quickly diminished as most orders were cancelled, causing thousands of workers to lose their jobs at Boeing. By the mid-1950s technology had advanced significantly, which gave Boeing the opportunity to develop and manufacture new products. One of the first was the short-range guided missile used to intercept enemy aircraft. At that time the Cold War was a fact and Boeing used the technology of these short-range missiles to develop intercontinental missiles.

Along with the development of these new products, the company tried to recover from the slowdown in demand by developing commercial aircraft that would be powered by turbofans instead of propellers, and could cross the Atlantic Ocean, but of course, by that time, the late 50s, aviation had grown globally and there were already factories around the world capable of implementing large models in an aeronautical market in constant growth and constant demand.

Transatlantic flights were the target of large factories and their successful models such as the British De Havilland Comet, the French Sud Aviation Caravelle and the Soviet Tupolev Tu-104. Therefore, in 1958, Boeing created the 707, a four-engine aircraft, capable of carrying 156 passengers on a transatlantic route.

Because it made shorter trips and more comfortable trips, the 707 quickly won the hearts of passengers.

Boeing had managed to turn the market around again, and this time without the help of its main customer, the U.S. Army. Boeing's business plans were ambitious, they wanted to bring their new masterpiece to commercial airlines around the world, but unlike what the company wanted, the companies began to ask for different versions of the same Boeing 707, which by then had commercially defeated its main competitors, the British De Havilland Comet, the French Sud Aviation Caravelle and the Soviet Tupolev Tu-104.

Some companies asked for a smaller version for shorter flights, but with the same safety and performance features, it was so that Boeing decided to shorten the initial model of the 707 and created the Boeing 720. A reactor of similar characteristics, but of shorter dimensions than its older brother, the 707.

Boeing's capabilities to adapt its original version of the 707 became famous throughout the world. They offered a standard product with versions adaptable to the needs of each company. Because of this, the airlines demanded a larger model from Boeing, at which point its main competitor Douglas, had promised to build a larger aircraft and complied by launching the renowned Douglas DC-8 on the market. An aircraft of similar characteristics to those of the 707, and even in its shape and appearance.

Sources of the time claim that this unleashed the trade war for Boeing and its managers, although by then, the company was firmly consolidated as one of the best in the world. Months later, Boeing began the development of a more elongated model and in July 1959 flew the new version of the 707, called Boeing 707-320. With a change in its engines and an improvement in the comforts of the passenger cabin, the new Boeing model generated many expectations, to such an extent that the company decided to launch an even larger aircraft on the market, in order to ensure that the competition could not match them. Shortly after the first flight of the 707-320, the company launched its latest version, the Boeing 707-420.

The model was followed by the 727 trijet and the 737 twinjet, becoming the world's best-selling commercial aircraft in the late twentieth century. Let's start by getting to know an emblem of the company, the Boeing 727.

On December 5, 1960, Boeing began construction of a new model that promised to perform short- and medium-range flights, with the ability to take off and land on "short" runways compared to the operational requirements of its predecessor, the Boeing 707. Initially, the 727 model had to go through a process of designs, drawings and several questions to be answered, as it is a new aircraft for a certain audience.

The design of the 727 was due to an agreement between the main airlines of the United States (United Airlines, American Airlines and Eastern Airlines) to look for a successor to the Boeing 707, a model that had marked a milestone in the history of the company. United Airlines wanted a four-engine aircraft for its flights to high-altitude airports, American was looking for a twin-engine aircraft for efficiency reasons while Eastern wanted a tri-engine for its flights over the Caribbean Sea. Finally, the three airlines coincided in a trimotor and thus the 727 was born. From this question comes the saying that the Boeing 727 was not an idea of Boeing but an idea of the three largest airlines in the United States.

Boeing engineers were facing a real challenge, they had to build an aircraft similar to the Boeing 707 but of completely different performance, more efficient, safer and with greater comforts than their, until then star plane. Nearly 70 different design projects were known on which Boeing had to make a decision and venture to start production.

For the final decision, factors such as the capacity of a high cruising speed at low altitude, low operating costs, high frequency in takeoff and landing cycles, a limited time between flight and flight and the possibility of reducing the noise of the turbines to enable operations in airports near urban areas were taken into account. As additional improvements, the Boeing 727 featured a "T" tail, an auxiliary power unit known as APU and ladders that allowed operation at airports where passenger services did not exist.

To all this, the recent direct competitor of Boeing and its 707 was still Douglas with its DC line. With the launch of Boeing's new model, the B727, Douglas decided to launch a similar version on the market in 1963, but aimed at a different market, in order to abandon the race with his competitor and work in parallel to him. At that time put into flight the new Douglas DC 9, a modern twin-engine narrow fuselage designed for short range and extremely economical operations for airlines.

The production line of the Boeing 727 continued until 1984 when it ended its era with a record 1830 units manufactured and delivered to the main airlines of the world. A record that the company held for years and that can only be reached by the mythical Boeing 737. The latest version of the B727 was an advanced version equipped with a flight computer that analysed performance improving the safety and efficiency of operations.

The new era

With the advent of jet engines, a new era had arrived for global aviation. This new way of building aircraft would not replace the traditional engines powered by huge propellers but would start a new stage in the manufacture of aircraft in different models.

By the end of the '60s, the aeronautical industry had advanced in such a way that no one considered that it could reach beyond what already existed. The great pioneers continued to manufacture innovative aircraft powered by jet engines as the newest on the market and with a continuous manufacture of engines propelled by traditional propellers. On these two variants of power plants, the large manufacturers varied their models in passenger capacity, autonomy, short, medium and long-range performance.

The trade war had become an inordinate struggle between the major commercial airlines. In the main market, the United States, the airline PANAM increased aircraft to its fleet steadily and required its main supplier, Boeing, to design and build new models that make a difference. It was then in the late 1960s that the factory released its two masterpieces, the B737 and the B747! Let's learn the history of each of these Boeing emblems.

Boeing 737

In the era of the aeronautical revolution of new aircraft with better power plants, better performance and greater capacity than the aircraft of the previous decade, the industry demanded constant progress from its operators. Thus, the first commercial battle to obtain this new Boeing model was not won by an American company, but by the German airline Lufthansa by anticipating the PANAM company in the purchase of the first model of the new Boeing 737. On February 19, 1965, Boeing announced its intention to build the MODEL 737, a short-range transport powered by two turbofans. The

The new B737 model consisted of the fuselage of the Boeing 727 with a tail configuration similar to the Boeing 707. A capacity of 60 to 85 passengers was envisaged, but Lufthansa, which placed the first order, needed a capacity of 100 seats. Because of this the fuselage was lengthened conveniently. The wing incorporated much of the technology developed for the 727 and the area of greatest changes was given by the powerplant. It was decided to mount the engines on the wing because there was no space in the short fuselage and because passengers cannot sit near the fuselage mounted engines.

Two months after Boeing launched the 737, the company announced the simultaneous development of the higher-capacity 737-200 model. The first 737-200 flew on August 8, 1967 and entered service with United Airlines on April 29, 1968. The 737-200 had the fuselage 1.83 m (6 ft) longer than the previous model to accommodate 130 passengers.

The rapid growth of air traffic, and therefore of the capabilities of aircraft at that time, meant that there was virtually no demand for the 737-100 (100-103 seats) so production ended after only 30 units had been built.

The 737's relatively short takeoffs and landings made it suitable for operating from small regional airports, and even from unpaved airfields. That's why Boeing developed appropriate FOD (Foreign Object Damage) protection for aircraft. The years were on and it seemed that the new model of the Boeing firm was going to surpass all the records foreseen and reached by previous models and the competition. Although the first commercial conquest of the B737 was in the hands of Lufthansa, the first symbolic achievement was of the United Airlines company who managed to buy the model of B737 number 100 built by the factory.

After its new model B737-200, Boeing launches a more advanced version known as B737-200 Advanced. This new version launched in 1979 had a greater autonomy, greater takeoff weight, was built with composite materials and equipped with the most advanced avionics system of the time.

Already in the decade of the '80, Boeing decides to give more life to its line of B737 and launches the new series of 737 known as Boeing 737 Classic. This series is composed of three emblems of the firm, the B737-300, the B737-400 and the B737-500.

They were characterized by having new technologies such as: New CFM-56 turbofan engines, which were 20% more efficient than the JT8D, used in the original version. Redesigned wings, improvements in aerodynamics, improvements in the cockpit, with the option of adding the EFIS system (Electronic Flight Instrumentation System, for its acronym in English). The passenger cabin similar to that used on the Boeing 757. The maximum speed for which this type of aircraft reaches the transonic regime is the critical Mach number, whose approximate value was 0.8M.

For its part, the legendary B737-200, already with too much history on its back and with a technology that was becoming obsolete in the face of so much progress in the industry, the 200 production ended in 1988 after having manufactured 1,114 units. The decade of the '80s had been a great success for the B737 saga in its Classic version. With worldwide sales records, the factory continued to build models and with an aeronautical market in constant growth, it was in 1993 that Boeing returned to give to talk. In that same year he launched the new series of the B737 named as B737 Next Generation. A new series of models that included the B737-600, B737-700, B737-800 and B737-900.

It is characterized by having new technologies such as: Update of the CFM-56-7 engines, being 7% more effective than the series 3 used in the classic line. The wings completely redesigned, increasing their width and area, among other improvements. Increase in fuel storage capacity, and also increase in maximum take-off weight. New redesigned cockpit, with 6 LCD screens along with the latest avionics technology. Passenger cabin upgrades, improved range and optimized for international travel.

The years followed their natural course and the success of the B737 Next Generation saga had no limits. Already in a market with greater competition from other large manufacturers such as Airbus and the A320 Family line, the production of the B737 demanded greater agility in deliveries, lower manufacturing cost and greater results in flight performances.

The fight between elite manufacturers had become a two-way fight, there was no other manufacturer that could compete with the B737 saga and the A320 line. Among them was the battle. Both firms improved their models year after year, seeking to obtain some competitive advantage over their competition. The aeronautical industry was no longer so young, the year 2000 had arrived and soon after the first 100 years of aviation life arrived. A cycle of experiences, mistakes and learnings that led manufacturers to perfect their techniques and equipment more and more every day.

Since 2006, the Boeing company had been studying different proposals to replace its Boeing 737 model, in a project called Boeing Y1, which would accompany the Boeing 787 Dreamliner. The decision on the launch of this program was postponed, being delayed until 2011. However, in 2010, Airbus launched the Airbus A320 Neo, a variant derived from the original A320, which incorporated a new, more efficient powerplant that featured lower operating costs. This decision was well received by numerous airlines, which placed numerous orders for this new aircraft. This caused Boeing's board of directors to approve on August 30, 2011, a renewal project with which to compete with Airbus, called Boeing 737 MAX.

Boeing claimed that the 737 MAX offered 16% lower fuel consumption than current Airbus A320 aircraft and 4% lower than the Airbus A320 Neo. The three models of the new variant were the 737 MAX 7, the 737 MAX 8 and the 737 MAX 9, which were based on the 737-700, 800 and 900ER respectively, which in turn were the best-selling models of the 737 Next Generation range.

That new artwork that the factory made available to the aviation industry has been a new demonstration that Boeing has the right tools and vision for the needs of the industry.

First flight
of the world's newest short-range jetliner!

Since its inception in 1965, the B737 has been a flagship aircraft for Boeing, year after year, decade after decade and it was 46 years after its first flight that this maximized version was born in order to show the world that the B737 model will remain in force for many more decades.

Boeing 747

The year was 1968 and with the new model of B737, the aeronautical industry had taken a big step in the so-called "Revolution of the airplanes". The aeronautical markets were increasingly demanding. The airlines requested constant improvements and updates of the models they offered to the market. The general public, who at the beginning of this revolution were somewhat shy about traveling by plane, was giving the new way of traveling a second chance. This made the demands of the public make the companies develop new projects, who were running an excessive race in a competition to be the leading airline in the market.

Thus, on September 30, 1968, thousands of people gathered at Boeing's new plant in Everett, about 50 kilometers from Seattle, to learn about the radical new design of the leading company until then in the manufacture of new models. However, the project of an aircraft of enormous dimensions was not Boeing's own initiative, but one of its customers. It all started from the office of the head of the airline Pan Am, who had realized that the constant demand was increasing by leaps and bounds, and although there was an increase in the number of flights, the planes could only carry a relatively small number of passengers.

A larger aircraft could help airlines cut costs, the Pan Am boss is asking Boeing to design something completely different: a "Super Airplane" that doubles the size of its 707 model, so far the company's commercial star. The new aircraft will become synonymous with the glamour of long haul travel. It will redefine the shape and size of airports and become a critical vehicle for freight forwarding companies. It will become a recognized name thanks to a play on words that refers to its enormous size: they will call it the Jumbo Jet. But, at least for Boeing, it will be the 747.

The history of this aircraft began with a little-known military project. In March 1964, the U.S. Air Force needed a large cargo plane so it asked construction companies to submit their proposals. The aircraft was to be capable of carrying about 52 tons of cargo over distances of 8,000 kilometers. In addition, it had to be so wide as to be able to accommodate a tank inside and had to have entry and exit ramps in the front and rear.

The competition for the design was won by the company Lockheed Martin, but the plan developed by Boeing would end up influencing an aircraft with a very different purpose. Considering all the caveats of the new project, Boeing engineer Joe Sutter planned a giant aircraft inspired by the demands of the military contract and the desire of the Pan Am executive to have a plane that would reduce congestion at airports.

Talking to potential customers like Pan Am, Sutter realized that airlines needed a plane that could carry far more than the 190 passengers that fit on the 707. Higher capacity would mean a lower cost per passenger. But there was an additional difficulty. At the time, Boeing was working on a more ambitious project, a supersonic aircraft that was supposed to compete with the Concorde. It was then thought that when those aircraft entered service, people would not want to fly in subsonic aircraft.

Considering that perhaps the new B747 would have more service life carrying cargo than passengers, the new Jumbo Jet had to maintain the same cargo aircraft configuration, with the cockpit above the passenger cabin, due to the idea that its days as a passenger aircraft were numbered. Making sure that the 747 could be a good cargo aircraft had a great influence on the design, which was born as a cargo plane and would become the most successful passenger aircraft in the world.

The company's challenge didn't end in just achieving the desired design. Before they could build the 747, Boeing had something else on its to-do list: building a factory big enough to assemble it. The plane was so large (it was 70.6 meters long and 59 meters wide) that it could not be built at any of Boeing's existing plants. Not only were they building one of the largest aircraft, but they were also building the largest building on the planet to assemble it. The Everett plant remains today one of the largest enclosed buildings in the world.

In February 1969 the first exhibition flight was made, during which it was shown that the Jumbo Jet could fly. But were the airlines interested in acquiring it? Pan Am was the main customer. Boeing had promised them to make the first delivery in late 1969, so the aircraft had to be designed and built in 28 months, rather than taking the usual 42 months required by a passenger plane. Other airlines were also interested, including British Airways, Lufthansa, Qantas, American Airlines and Delta.

In principle there had been some resistance to the 747, especially from some U.S. airlines. In the U.S., worried that most airports would not be able to receive it. Boeing was convinced that companies operating transatlantic flights would see the benefits of such a large aircraft. A big point in its favor was the fact that it could carry up to 550 passengers, almost four times more than the 707. On January 15, 1970, the first 747-100 (the first model to enter service) was officially christened by the first lady of the United States, Pat Nixon.

Despite the festive atmosphere of such an event, the difficulties were not yet over. Boeing was heavily indebted by the time and the United States went into recession. Each model of the 747 cost $24 million (the equivalent of $155 million in 2020) and the company only managed to sell two units for a year and a half.

Some companies that had been interested in buying it quickly opted to order smaller planes in the face of the rising cost of fuel after the 1973 oil crisis. Other customers found that the expected reduction in costs per passenger of the 747 only occurred if the ship flew full since with 70% occupancy it spent almost the same amount of fuel as with all seats sold. Boeing needed the 747 to be a success, so it t adjusted the design by listening to the airlines' suggestions.

There were Japanese companies that wanted to have as many seats as possible (550) to use on shorter journeys, so Boeing made a version that could carry less fuel and more luggage, so the 747-200 was born, equipped with more powerful engines and capacity to take off carrying more weight.

As more companies began placing orders, the 747 became synonymous with a long-haul luxury flight in the 1970s and 1980s. To attract more passengers, some airlines took advantage of the ample cabin space to offer luxuries never before imagined. American Airlines, for example, included a piano bar in economy class; while those at Continental had a lounge room with sofas.

American Airlines New 747 LuxuryLiner
The Plane With No Competition

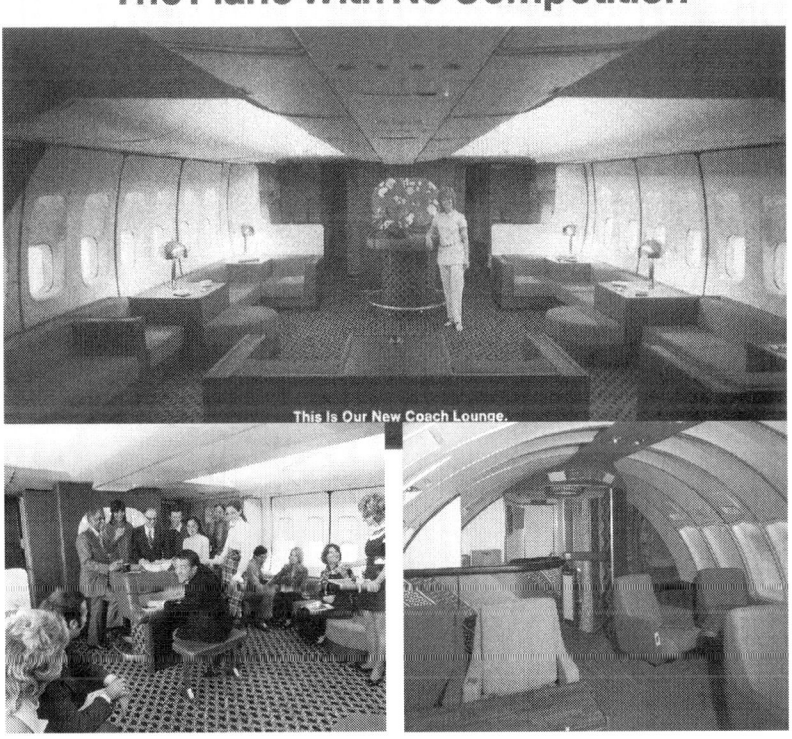

Already in the mid-80s, the model was a great success. Cathay Pacific airline had led the B747 to record maximum range records on international routes. Cathay had the longest routes in the world, and had shown that the B747 was capable of flying from Hong Kong to Vancouver round trip. This led to Boeing sending a team to see what else they could do as the market was constantly growing and the demands of the airlines were increasing. The result was the 747-400 with engines made by Rolls Royce and released by Cathay Pacific.

The new 747-400 could fly about 14,200 kilometers loaded to full capacity. It was able to achieve this, in part, thanks to the addition of devices on the tips of its wings that improved its aerodynamics and allowed to save fuel. If the companies wanted, they could order versions in which they could carry 660 passengers in a single economy class. The first models took off in 1988 and many are still in operation.

The years passed and the Jumbo Jet continued to add fans. Companies around the world wanted it among their fleets. With time and modifications, the legendary B747 had become a "mandatory" aircraft for any airline that wanted to expand its borders to long-range flights and maximum capacity.

From the modifications of the new B747-400 the market had put all eyes on the performance that this new model would have. As expected, it was not a model that went unnoticed and quickly won over the general public. Every year there were more airlines that were encouraged to the adventure of incorporating their first Boeing 747-400, an aircraft came to expectations for its customers, both pilots, entrepreneurs and passengers in its entirety, who particularly aroused the curiosity of how it could be better than the legendary B747 previous. Its technology, its sound reduction, its performance and its comforts were the main stars of this new model that managed to conquer the international market again.

The turn of the millennium was approaching and Boeing executives had big plans for their company. Among them and perhaps one of the most ambitious was the relaunch of the mythical B747-400 with two versions for the first decade of the new millennium, a superior version intended for passenger flight and a modified version, completely dedicated to cargo transport, a market that Boeing had never left aside and that had started the line of the legendary Boeing 747.

Thus, in 2005, Boeing announced the launch of the new 747-800 model. It was developed from the Boeing 747-400, with fuselage lengthened by 5.65 meters, innovative wings and improved efficiency. For the first time, Boeing offered a model to be used in cargo transport from the beginning, instead of using used aircraft that were eliminated in the passenger cabin in the last stage of their useful life.

By then, the 747 was no longer the only jumbo jet. Airbus, Boeing's European rival, had designed a large-capacity aircraft: the A380, which could carry up to 853 passengers, but we will know its history in the chapter corresponding to the "History of Airbus". Driven by the A380's enormous competition, the Jumbo jet was no longer alone in the skies. In this context, Boeing had to surprise the market again with a new model of one of its star aircraft, but this time, the new model would not be alone and would be tested with a competitor worthy of recognition.

It was from the hand of one of his new projects, the Boeing 787 "Dream Liner", that the new version of the B747 was born. It was 2006 and Boeing's plans were very clear, they had to run along with the competition (Airbus) and revolutionize the market again with a new long-range twin-engine model and the latest generation in technologies, performance and comfort. This is how the Boeing 787 project was born and depending on the needs of this new model, the need arose for a cargo aircraft superior to the B747-800 that is capable of moving the parts and components of the new B787 model. In order to meet this need, the Boeing 747-400 LCF (large cargo freighter) "DreamLifter" was born. The figures proposed by this new work of art by Boeing were really impressive, almost 22 meters high (like a five-story building) more than 1,800 cubic meters of capacity, three times the load capacity of a 747-400, a cruising speed close to 900 km / h and capacity to supply 250,000 liters of fuel. While the "DreamLifter" was not an aircraft that the company built to be marketed, its launch again revolutionized the aeronautical market.

Today, the "DreamLifter" is part of Boeing's own fleet as a model manufactured exclusively for transporting parts of the company's aircraft, its own cargo aircraft, customized and custom designed. A "taste" that only a Boeing company could give.

While there are no known new Boeing projects on its flagship model, it will surely be a model that will last for many more years. To date, new technologies have led long-range twin-engines to cover all the needs that the legendary B747 used to cover in all its versions, but there is still a market that depends exclusively on these huge flying machines, the air cargo market.

Boeing 787

With the beginning of the new century came a new era of aircraft to the aeronautical market. The B787 model is the "Spoiled Child of Boeing", its youngest model, but with a proposal of innumerable commercial benefits. The project began in the late '90s when the company was trying to take a big step in the market with two very promising projects, a new B747X and a new model known as Sonic Cruiser, which would stand out for flying faster than any aircraft on the market obtaining 15% more speed than the rest of its competitors.

This new version faster than the rest of the models, promised a great competitive advantage by being able to offer a reduction in operating times without a significant increase in consumption, since it was expected to have the same fuel consumption as its similar model the Boeing 767.

In January 2005 the 787 was known by the development designation 7E7. By April of the following year, Boeing had its design ready to be presented in society. With a less daring nose and a more conventional tail, the final design presented a much superior aerodynamics to the rest of the known models.

The aviation industry had suffered a severe setback following the attacks of 11 September 2001 and rising oil prices, so airlines began to focus more on efficiency than speed. This shift in the aviation market caused Boeing to cancel the Sonic Cruiser project it was working on. In a change of course, the company announced an alternative product using Sonic Cruiser technology, but employing a more conventional configuration, dubbed the 7E7.

r The replacement of the Sonic Cruiser project was given the nickname "7E7" (although internally Boeing called it "Y2"). The technology from the Sonic Cruiser and 7E7 was to be used as part of a Boeing project that would replace the company's entire range of passenger aircraft, a program known as project Yellowstone, and of which the 7E7 was the first part of it. Several media speculated that the "E" meant several things, such as "efficiency" or "ecological", although in the end Boeing said that this letter meant "eight" (in English: "eight"). In July 2003, a public competition was held to give the aircraft a name, from which the name Dreamliner emerged. Other popular names that also had the possibility of being voted were eLiner, Global Cruiser or Stratoclimber.

The 787 was designed to become the first composite airliners to be mass-produced, in which the fuselage would be joined in single-piece cylindrical sections instead of the multiple layers of aluminium and the nearly 50,000 rivets used in aircraft at the time.

Boeing claimed that the 787 would be an aircraft that brought a 20% improvement in fuel consumption over the 767, of which about 40% of the increase in energy efficiency came from the new power plants, plus the benefits derived from aerodynamic improvements, the increase in the use of lighter materials and in the application of new systems.

By 2006, Boeing had almost ready its first production batch of the new model, but unforeseen events arose that delayed the launch. Boeing stated in December 2006 that the first six 787s were overweight, with the forecast that the first six aircraft were 5,000 pounds (2268 kg) heavier than anticipated. As stated, the 787-9's curb weight exceeded 14,000 pounds (6350.3 kg).

The seventh aircraft would be the first in the 787-8 series to meet weight targets. As part of this slimming process, Boeing redesigned some parts and made greater use of titanium.

The years passed without novelty of a date planned for the first flight of the new model. Boeing had repeatedly announced delays in launch dates due to delays in the delivery of materials for assembly.

It took nearly five years until the first of the serial 787-8s was officially delivered to Japanese airline All Nippon Airways in September 2011 at Boeing's Everett, Washington, facility.

In October of the same year, the 787-8 made its first commercial flight, on a flight operated by the airline "All Nippon Airways" that went from Tokyo International Airport to Hong Kong International Airport.

Tickets for this first flight were sold in an online auction, which reached the maximum bid of $ 34,000 for a seat on that first flight. Boeing fans around the world wanted to belong to the company's history by becoming the first passengers to fly in its momentous new model.

Chapter 2

The History of AIRBUS

The History of Airbus

Today, Airbus is the leading company in the commercial aircraft sales market. In a very short period of life, unlike its main competitor the Boeing company, Airbus has achieved a record sales and leads the fleets of the largest companies in the world. Its history began at the end of 1969 where the governments of the United Kingdom, France and Germany sought to unify concepts and created an aircraft of greater dimensions and performance than the Boeing fleet until that time. An ambitious project, but working together they managed to make it possible.

By the mid-1960s, the respective countries had begun preliminary negotiations with different companies. Each company already had this goal; in 1959 the Hawker Siddeley company had announced a version of the "Amstrong Whitworth AW660" that could accommodate a large number of passengers on ultra-short routes for about 2 pounds per seat and mile.

However, European aircraft manufacturers were aware of the risks of such a development and began to accept, together with their governments, that collaboration was necessary for the development of such aircraft and to compete with the most powerful American manufacturers. At the 1965 Paris air show, major European airlines informally discussed their requirements for the new model, capable of carrying 100 passengers or more over short and medium distances at low cost.

Years passed and in 1969 the British government withdrew its support for the program. The French and Germans were unable to continue alone, but eventually managed to continue with another German financial backing. The first project they would plan would be that of a European multinational commercial aircraft. Its creation was not easy, but finally Germany and France agreed and in May 1969 they signed the agreement to start the project that they would call Airbus 300 or A300B (name that came from the promise an aircraft capable of transporting 300 people).

The Airbus name was an ownerless term used by the aviation industry in the 1960s to refer to a commercial aircraft of a certain size, so it was accepted by the French language. Perhaps unknowingly, by signing that agreement, they were giving life to one of the largest companies in the world and a leader in the manufacture of aircraft, not only commercial, but also cargo and military. A year after the signing of the contract, in December 1970, "Airbus Industrie" was officially founded with the legal figure of a groupement d'intérêt économique (GIE), an institution similar to a consortium. By then the A300 manufacturing process had already begun and with it was the new series of aircraft, the A300 family, to be born.

Airbus A300

On October 20, 1972, the new European model with a wide-body and two-large engines made its official presentation. He left the hangars of Toulouse before the watchful eye of a large number of public, including executives of the firm, authorities of the countries involved, dozens of photographers, and the general public. There it was, the great European plane presenting itself in society.

In total by the end of 1973, the four A300B1 prototypes and two more in production, A300B2 (6 in total), were already in flight, which obtained their international certification on May 30, 1974.
That same day, the first two Airbus A300B2 series, were delivered in a large ceremony with the presence of the heads of state, to the French company Air France, to inaugurate the Paris - London route.

Everything seemed to be going well for Airbus, however, the path of the Airbus A300 would not be a simple path to travel. Despite the good reviews of the international media, just in those years the famous oil "crisis" was being experienced, which had led to the bankruptcy of several companies in the sector.

In 1976, Airbus' results could not be more discouraging, in one year only one aircraft had been sold. But this crisis had something in favor of Airbus and that was that this aircraft had been designed to face the problem of consumption and be more efficient with lower operating costs, generating a huge competitive advantage over the large American aircraft.

At the end of 1977, the American company Eastern Airlines, rented to Airbus, 4 A300B4 for a period of 6 months on trial, with an option to buy. And not only did he finally buy these 4 aircraft, but he also placed an order for another 34 more aircraft, since the A300B4 model consumed 30% less fuel than the rest of its competitors.

With this stroke of luck, things changed course substantially and several American companies such as American Airlines, US Airways, United Airlines, Delta Airlines, decided to operate this economical aircraft and placed their orders. By then, the new European aircraft had become a major competitor worldwide, managing to sell more than 800 A300 aircraft to more than 80 international companies in 45 countries.

The years passed and the A300s generated a furor in airlines around the world. Its performance, its performance, its economy and its new style of flying, made the A300 a first-line competition of the American mega company Boeing.

The success of the A300 reached not only passengers and operators but also the airlines that dominated the air freight market. The enormous dimensions of the A300 in load configuration, allowed operators to transport tens of tons without risk, economically and in record time. This earned the A300 its place as one of the most successful cargo aircraft in history.

The carrying capacity is incredible for the numbers that were considered at that time. The performance of the A300 freighter version gave Airbus the opportunity to expand into a market in which its main competitor, Boeing, was leading a long time ago.

The legendary A300 continued its course in a life cycle full of achievements and surrounded by commercial successes for its operators. With 843 examples sold, thousands of tons transported and millions of passengers transported, the first son of Airbus ended its life cycle in 2007 when the factory decided to close the production line of the A300/310 model. To this day, many airlines continue to use this legendary model as a cargo version due to its excellent dimensions and capabilities. A freighter model that marked a milestone in the history of cargo transport and that gave way to another milestone in the history of Airbus, the birth of an extravagant model that challenged all known designs, the "Airbus 300-600ST Beluga".

Airbus A300-600ST BELUGA

Already as an aircraft manufacturing company par excellence, Airbus had developed a business model where it manufactured every part of its aircraft in different countries in Europe. This allowed it to diversify risks and delays, maximizing production times, and even deducting operating costs. With the start of this new manufacturing model, the main problem was the transport of the different parts from each country to the Airbus assembly center. Initially, transports were carried out by land and sea, but the time and operational cost turned out to be a problem rather than a solution.

Looking for a solution to this problem, Airbus contacted its main competitor to request a solution among "colleagues" and Boeing proposed to operate its B377 Super Guppy selling 4 units to Airbus. This aircraft was a model that had belonged to NASA's Apollo space program. The attempt to solve the problem did not work since the Super Guppy were old models and high operating costs, added to the fact that their capacity was not enough for Airbus' plans.

Based on the growing need to find a solution to the problem of loading its aircraft components, Airbus needed to maximize the capabilities of Boeing's Super Guppy, and developed a similar model with capabilities superior to Boeing's model and exclusive for Internal Airbus Use. This made the rumors of copy that had flooded the market, clear since Airbus had no intentions of marketing the model, but simply improving the version that had bought from Boeing to be able to solve its problem of logistics of parts.

Thus, in 1991 a company was created to develop this new model. From the twin-engine wide-body Airbus A300 the Beluga was developed. The wings, engines, landing gear and underbody were retained. The upper part of the fuselage was replaced by a horseshoe-shaped structure of 7.4 m in diameter. To allow access to the cargo cabin, the control cabin was brought to a lower level than the cargo cabin, and a 17 m high door was incorporated into the front of the aircraft. In addition, the tail structure was modified, which was elongated and widened, adding two additional vertical rudders, to improve the maneuverability and stability of the aircraft.

Although the start of production of the Beluga was in September 1992, the inaugural flight took a couple more years until September 13, 1994. The model obtained airworthiness certification a year later. In total five Belugas were built for the sole purpose of carrying the components of Airbus aircraft from production sites to final assembly lines, but they are also available for special cargo jobs, such as the transfer of components from the International Space Station, large works of art, industrial machinery, or entire helicopters.

Since its inception, the Beluga has met all the expectations of Airbus operational and is still valid to meet the company's demanding needs. Today, the transport of huge cargo is no longer a problem for Airbus. While the Beluga is a young aircraft with limited production of only five examples, the factory has made constant improvements and updates to continue expanding the potential of this huge freighter to what is now known as the latest version, the Beluga XL.

Airbus A310

Going back to the beginnings of the A300, the demands of the operators were covered by the Airbus models, but the constant demand of the passengers and new routes, made the demands of the companies increasingly strict in terms of the costs and performance of the aircraft. Due to the requirements of the airlines that put Airbus at the top of the market, who complained that the A300 was too big for certain routes, the factory created a model surpassing the already successful A300, the new and more modern A310.

The Airbus A310 is a derivative of the Airbus A300, its main differences being the shortened fuselage, redesigned wings and a smaller horizontal stabilizer. This new model made its maiden flight in April 1983 and Lufthansa was the first airline to operate the new model.

While the A310 model was an Airbus response to the specific needs of the market, it was not considered a successful model. Only 255 units were manufactured unlike its older brother, the legendary A300 that exceeded 800 units sold. Within that amount put into service by Airbus, different versions were modified, improving the maximum takeoff weight, flight technology, performance and performance in general.

Beyond the A310 was part of the A300 range and was overshadowed by the success of its predecessor, it was an aircraft that framed Airbus forever. With it, the idea of simplifying the flight operation in each model of the so-called A300 Family arose, which led to the creation of an aircraft model that could be simple in operation and similar to its previous model. This would give A300 pilots the ability to make a very agile and dynamic transition from one model to another. This concept of homogeneity had led Airbus to modify its designs and flight concepts, thus achieving that all its next models are similar in operational characteristics. Today it is a concept that is more valid than ever. An A320 pilot has the operational know-how to make a reduced training transition and be able to fly the huge A380. All this thanks to the development of the "Airbus Operational Philosophy".

With this new model in flight and a new operational philosophy, Airbus was ready to once again lead the market with one of its elite aircraft that would mark commercial aviation forever. The "A320 Family" aircraft saga is born.

Airbus A320

It all started in June 1981, when Airbus announced the launch of the Airbus A320 design programme. With the design based on single-aisle aircraft with capacity for more than 100 passengers, it was the European bet to combat the B727, B737 and the MD DC-9 that already triumphed on the part of the American manufacturer, Boeing. It was not until 1984, when thanks to Air France placing a firm order for 50 units, that the development program was truly officially launched. During the first years of production, 100 firm orders were reached, including some American airlines.

It was 1987 when the first test flight arrived. It was a flight commanded by Airbus pilots and engineers who formed a crew of six. It was the big moment for Airbus. All of Europe would be watching the aeronautical event of the year and Airbus had accustomed its public to dazzle in its exhibitions.

A year later, in February 1988 came the certification that allowed him to fly commercially. So it was that just a month later, Air France was in charge of inaugurating in regular flight, the entry into service of the first A320.

After the inaugural flight of Air France, all of Europe continued to observe closely this new model that had arrived at the right time where there was an aeronautical euphoria of the general public. So much so, that the postal service of Germany published a stamp in honor of such an event in order to honor the work of its people, remembering that parts of the A320 were built in Germany.

The new A320 could carry 150 passengers 3,440 km away. Its A320-200 version would later incorporate a central fuel tank that would allow it to increase its capacity from 15,590 liters to 23,450 liters, thus making it possible to increase the range to 5280 km. The A320 also had an internal diameter of its fuselage of 3.7 m, above the 3.45 m of the B737, which increased the comfort of passengers at the cost of increasing their weight. To compensate for the overweight, the wing had to be re-designed to provide greater aerodynamic efficiency. The result was a wing with a 25° arrow optimized to fly at Mach 0.82.

The success of the new model traveled the world showing its benefits and special characteristics that differentiated it from its competitors. The A320 was the first aircraft in its category to introduce a composite structure, a containerized loading system or the centralized maintenance and diagnostics system; it was also the first aircraft to incorporate the sidestick known as "Fly By Wire". A somewhat revolutionary system for the time where commands mechanically linked to control surfaces was the only option.

With all its improvements in subsequent versions, the A320 knew how to win the trust of the most prestigious companies in the world market. This fact made Airbus see the need to maximize the capabilities of its new model and achieve versions adaptable to all the needs of each particular company, but maintaining the A320 line and its resounding success. This is how more members were incorporated into the A320 family, such as the elongated version (A321) in 1994, and the smaller ones: A319 (1996) and A318 (2003), and helped, without a doubt, Airbus to achieve operating profits in 1991 for the first time in its history.

Airbus A321

The A321 emerged as an elongated version of the A320 (6.95 m more), and provided up to 25% more passenger capacity, incorporating small modifications to the wing such as double-slot flaps, minor changes in the leading edge or an increased wing surface from the 124 M2 of the A320 to 128 M2. The new model also needed to reinforce its landing gear to accommodate the additional 9600 Kg of take-off weight to reach 83 tons of MTOW. The german company Lufthansa was in charge of releasing the new model in 1994 and together with the premiere of the new model of its fleet, the following year it changed the paint design of its aircraft, achieving a more modern model for the time and in comparison they are the presentation of the A320.

Airbus A319

The A319 was announced in June 1993 during the Paris Air Show as a direct competitor to the B737-300/700, with its first flight being in August 1995. It had the same cockpit as the A320, which allowed A320 pilots to fly it with minimal adaptive training. It was a version 3.73 m shorter than the A320, which had allowed the number of emergency doors to be reduced from six to only two on the wings. With virtually the same fuel capacity as the A320-200, the same engines (but with less power) and only 124 passengers, the A319 offered a range of 6,650 km. A version that sought to adapt to the needs where the A320 models turned out to be too large and expensive for low-end operations.

Eager to try to monopolize the market for executive flights, a market that was being exploited on a large scale by Boeing, Airbus engineers proposed an exclusive version of the A319 where the buyer could opt for different configurations inside. It is an executive

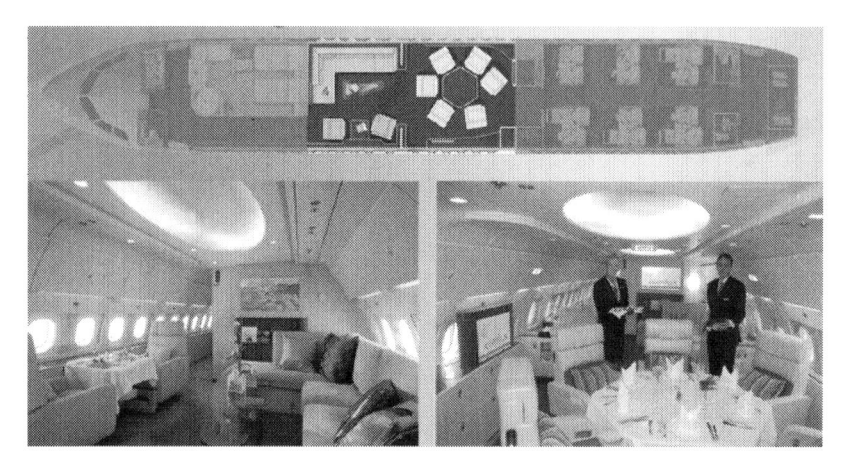

The history of the A319 would not end in its Business Jet. With the success and acceptance it had in the market, Airbus decided to bet on more and try to cover a market that had left aside with the manufacture of commercial aircraft, the military market. Thus, in 2002 the firm proposed an aircraft with characteristics similar to commercial ones, but adapted to maritime patrols. Hence the idea of

Airbus to bring to the market a military version of its successful A319, the Airbus 319 MPA (Maritime Patrol Aircraft).

Airbus A318

Originally designed to meet the needs posed by Chinese companies, in April 1999 the project of the smallest model of the Airbus family was announced. It proposed a capacity of about 100 passengers and a maximum range of 5,700.

Despite some last-minute inconveniences with its engines, the A318 was entered into service in January 2002. Quite a challenge for Airbus, considering that the global aviation environment was terrified by the attacks of September 11, 2001. However, this did not discourage the capabilities of the young child in the family and came to light in early 2002.

It was an extremely small model, to which they attributed some jokes for its size but that its operational capabilities managed to put its public on its feet when it was certified by the European authorities to make approaches of high slopes in extreme airports where the A320 was seen with serious operational problems. The anecdote of this small but great Airbus model was that its manufacture coincided in time with the design of the A380, so Airbus designers found themselves working simultaneously with their largest aircraft ever built while designing the smallest ever built.

Airbus A320 Neo

It was the end of 2010 when Airbus officially launched the upgrade program of its most successful model in history, the A320. A model that headed the A320 family but that was time to relaunch the market, a market that demanded less fuel consumption, less noise pollution, more comforts and greater range at lower cost. Four years after its announcement, on September 25, 2014, Airbus test pilots and engineers made the first test flight of their new model, which promised a reduction in consumption by 16% compared to the previous A320, 2 tons more maximum weight and almost 1000 KM more range than its predecessor.

Everything seemed to indicate that the new model of the A320 would bring a sum of successes for Airbus. Thus, the A320Neo model gave Airbus the record of having completed the largest sale of a commercial aircraft to the same company with the modest amount of 300 aircraft in a single order made by the company IndiGo, one of the largest in India. A multimillion-dollar transaction of 29,800 million Euros that put Airbus on another commercial level.

Despite this record order, IndiGo failed to take the privilege of making the first flight of the new A320 Neo. The honor was scheduled for Virgin America in September 2016, but was changed to Qatar Airways for bidding reasons. Unfortunately Qatar rejected its first order for the new model and the privilege of the inaugural flight was taken again by Lufthansa. IndiGo Airlines was the second airline to operate the new A320Neo.

Airbus A330 y A340

As Airbus continued to grow and expand its aircraft offering, on the other side of the world, Boeing continued to create successes and boasted of the benefits of one of its most profitable aircraft, the Boeing 767, a twin-engine wide-body that allowed intercontinental flights with record numbers of passengers. In order to compete with this market segment, at the end of 1987, Airbus launched a program of manufacturing two models in parallel, both wide-body and with capabilities superior to those that the B767 had shown to possess, with the difference that Airbus would go on the market with a twin-engine wide-body aircraft and a similar but four-engine aircraft.

Based on the company's successful model, the A300, Airbus sought to maximize the qualities of this, modernizing the cockpit, improving range and reducing consumption compared to its direct competitor the B767. The A330-300, the first version of this aircraft, made its first flight in November 1992 and entered service with the French airline Air Inter in January 1994. In response to declining sales, Airbus released a slightly shorter version, the A330-200, in 1998, with which it achieved greater sales success.

Other variants of the A330 were subsequently developed, including the A330-200F cargo aircraft, and the A330 MRTT military tanker.

It was the turn of the older brother of the series, the four-engine A340. Airbus manufactured the A340 in four different fuselage lengths. It was officially unveiled on 25 October 1991 in one of the hangars on the Airbus assembly line.

It was the turn of the older brother of the series, the four-engine A340. Airbus manufactured the A340 in four different fuselage lengths. It was officially unveiled on 25 October 1991 in one of the hangars on the Airbus assembly line.

Launch customers Lufthansa and Air France put the A340 into service in March 1993.

As of September 2011, airlines had ordered a total of 379 examples of the A340. The most widely used model was the A340-300, with 218 examples delivered, while Lufthansa was the largest operator of the A340, with 64 aircraft purchased. Airbus announced on 10 November 2011 that it was ending the A340 programme due to a lack of new orders. The A340 became one of the world's most popular long-range aircraft among passengers. But commercially it did not have the expected sales success, and little by little it was retiring from the skies of the world. When Airbus ceased production, the new generation of twin-engine models built in composite materials already reigned, which had a lower fuel consumption that made it more attractive than this powerful aircraft.

Airbus A380

The beginnings of the world's largest aircraft did not happen in the first decade of the 2000s as most believe. The ambitious project of creating the largest aircraft on the planet was on the minds of major airlines as early as the late 80s when a group of Airbus engineers began working in secret on a project to develop a high-capacity aircraft in order to break Boeing's dominance with its B747. But Airbus was not the only company that had this dream, the American company McDonnell Douglas had similar plans, but with a much more advanced project that they called MD-12. A huge model of four engines and two floors of passenger cabins.

However, despite the similarities of the MD-12 with the A380 model, the scant support obtained from investors and the bad commercial statistics that did not provide a good picture, the MD-12 project was discarded by the firm. Knowing the failure of the MD-12, Airbus managers decided to continue with the project trying to build on the negative points that the project had presented from the competition, in order to improve them and overcome the proposed barriers. The new Airbus project was announced at the Farnborough Air Show with a letter of introduction that knew how to seduce future stakeholders, promising that the new design and performance of the new Airbus would reduce the operational cost by 15% in relation to its main competitor, the American giant B747.

Airbus put four teams of designers and engineers to work at the same time in order to find the ideal model and for each team to propose new methods and technologies in the design and construction of future aircraft. The designs were presented in 1992, with the most competitive design being chosen.

. With the project already underway and an official budget of 8,000 million dollars, in 1994 Airbus formally began the manufacture of its most ambitious model. The project already had a name and was known as the "A3XX" project. Several designs had been considered, including a combination of two fuselages, side by side, of the A340 which was at the time the largest aircraft built by the European company. The A3XX, a project already public knowledge, had to face different statistical challenges and the new aircraft that Boeing planned to develop from its 747 in order not to fall behind the A3XX project.

Airbus began by consulting major airlines and representatives of major international airports to establish the size of the aircraft in order to use existing airport facilities without the need for major renovations. The dimensions of each unit should not exceed 80 meters in length and wingspan, the maximum height was set at 24 m. These limitations were designed to allow the A380 to maneuver in the parking lots and streets of airports operating Boeing 747s.

Thus, in 1996, its main customer of always Air France proposed to Airbus actively in the project. To prepare for the arrival of the A3XX, Air France carried out a long work with the airport authorities in order to adapt the infrastructure and ground equipment. For example, the runways had to have a minimum width of 45 meters and the 516 passengers had to be able to comfortably board a 2-level aircraft. Specific training was also given to Air France crew and ground staff to adapt to the demands of this uncommon aircraft.

After completing all the preliminary work, Airbus was ready to start its production chain. For this, parts of different areas of Europe arrived, by land, sea and even by air with their own cargo plane, the Beluga. An incredible work of logistics and coordination so that everything worked perfectly in order to meet deadlines.

By having separate manufacturing and assembly plants in different parts of Europe, Airbus was able to accelerate production times and meet agreed delivery deadlines. But the most important thing was still missing, the official presentation to the world of its new model.

Little by little the giant was taking shape. All eyes of the aeronautical world were on the date of presentation. The largest airlines in the world wanted to have the privilege of making the first commercial flight of the largest aircraft in the world.

Airbus already had more than 100 official orders from Asian giants such as Qatar, Emirates, Air China among the main ones in the world. Europe's eyes were also on the new model, Air France, Lufthansa and British Airways had formal orders to Airbus for the immediate incorporation of the new model that was about to be born.

The official unveiling of the Airbus A380 took place on 18 January 2005 in a hangar on the company's final Jean-Luc Lagardère assembly line in Toulouse, France. His presentation brought together more than 5000 people. The ceremony lasted approximately two hours, during which time the 35 years of the European Airbus consortium and its successes since the launch of the Airbus 310 in the early 80s were commemorated.

The first aircraft was delivered on 15 October 2007 to Singapore Airlines, with which it entered service on 25 October 2007, on an inaugural flight between Singapore and Sydney. Passengers bought the tickets at a charity auction, with the price of each ticket hovering between $560 and $100,000.

Emirates Airlines was the second airline to take in the A380, on 28 July 2008, and made its maiden flight between Dubai and New York on 1 August 2008.

Airbus A350

The history of the Airbus A350 is born from the eternal struggle of the two giants such as Boeing and Airbus, who have constantly launched new products to the market in order to always be one step ahead of their competitor. With the intention of responding to the European company, Boeing had launched a new two-engine wide-body model under the name B767, to which Airbus responded with a chain series that it called the A330 and A340. Without being left behind, Boeing responded again with the creation of the wonderful and huge Boeing 777. This was the case for decades, where both companies showed their enormous capabilities to create new and wonderful aircraft in order to always be present in an aeronautical market that demanded more and more.

The pitched battle to lead the market did not reed and in April 2004, Boeing announced the program of the firm's new model, the Boeing 787. Eight months later, Airbus announced the launch of its most modern equipment, the A350, with promises of carbon fiber construction, Rolls Royce engines, more efficient wings and extremely improved fuel consumption. However, Airbus' announcement did not exceed expectations as the company had planned as the public observed the project as a modification of the A330, but improving its qualities.

It was not until 2006 that the A350 project began to sound in the aeronautical environment when at the Berlin air exhibition that same year, Airbus relaunched the project, but changing the concept and proposing a family of A350 XWB aircraft.

The A350 XWB (Xtra Wide Body) family proposed a revolutionary new model of wider fuselage than the previous one, with a greater amount of use of carbon fiber and a substantial improvement in the overall design. This business model had had excellent results with the A320 family and without a doubt, it was the first plan that the company now had. The radical change responded to the expectations and interests of the companies and it was only a matter of seeing the orders that arrived: 294 for the first year, 163 additional in 2008, being a total of 810 orders of the 3 models at the end of 2016.

The A350 XWB model should compete with Boeing's new 787, but also with the 777, the flagship product of the American company. The prototype n°1 of the future A350 flew for the first time on June 14, 2013, that is, 7 years after the start of the final project.

Qatar Airways, as the launch airline of the A350, was the first to accept and operate the aircraft, receiving its copy in its colours on 22 December 2014, and starting the inaugural flight between Doha and Frankfurt on 15 January 2015.

Motivated by the success of its A350 program, Airbus continued to seek to improve what until then already seemed unbeatable and on November 22, 2018 opened calls at the plants in Madrid and Toulouse to sign new engineers and designers and start working on the development of a variant of its latest model, the A350 NEO.

Today, the A350 XWB family has had the same success as its younger brother the fabulous A320 that is still reaping successes.

All airlines would like to have this revolutionary Airbus model among their fleets, but only the most prestigious ones have been indulge in and today they enjoy the benefits of a state-of-the-art aircraft with everything it has to have to lead the market. Similar to a fan's fanaticism with their favorite rock star, airlines crave their first photo with the new industry star.

Chapter 3

Presidential Aircrafts

Introduction

Presidential aviation has transported leaders of the highest power throughout the world. The most important governments on the planet choose these two companies (Airbus and Boeing) for the design and manufacture of the government aircraft that will transport their presidents. These very particular aircraft seem to be just another model of classic commercial aircraft, but they are endowed with countless additions that make the safety of these flying strengths.

Although they share the same main design as commercial aircraft, inside they are completely customized according to the requirements of each government. From missile evasion systems, to fully equipped military operating rooms. Everything, absolutely everything is customized according to what each operator requires. Exclusive and personalized furniture, rooms, meeting room, command center, kitchens, living rooms and all the necessary environments to replicate the presidential residences with the highest detail.

Two of the best known of these magnificent aircraft are the presidential plane of the United States government, a Boeing 747 (Air Force One) in different models, and the French presidential plane, an Airbus 330 known as "Cotam Unité". In this chapter we will learn in detail each of these magnificent models along with the most outstanding presidential planes from around the world.

United States presidential aircraft (Boeing)

All the presidents of the United States from 1943 onwards have chosen the Boeing company as the supplier of the presidential plane. Until 1959, this choice of manufacturers for such an important task was divided between Boeing and Douglas until, prior to the beginning of the 1960s, Boeing took over all the presidential transportation.

The first was the Boeing 314 Clipper known as the "flying boat" because of its ability to " perch on the water". Due to the outbreak of the World War, little was the use that this first presidential plane had since it was replaced by the following Douglas models until 1959 when Boeing strengthened its relationship with the government and introduced the first Air Force One, a Boeing 707 and exclusively dedicated to the transport of presidents. The relationship between the Boeing 707 models and the presidents of each era continued until 1990 when it was replaced by the current Boeing 747 through several models until today.

It was in 1990 under the presidency of HW Bush that this important model change took place and Boeing's new presidential plane, its flagship model, the Boeing 747-200, arrived.

This new model offered comforts that its predecessor could not because of its design, already at that time, was out of date. A section of common seats at the end of the aircraft, meeting room, presidential room and various sections made this model a portrait of the white house but in flight.

Since 1990, the presidential fleet has consisted of two aircraft specifically configured from the Boeing 747-200B series with the designation VC-25A. Although these aircraft are known as Air Force One while the president is on board, the term is commonly used to describe any of the three presidential aircraft normally used and maintained by the United States Air Force exclusively to transport the president.

Aircraft that serve as Air Force One differ from the common Boeing 747s in size, characteristics, and safety measures. With 370 m2 of interior space, they include multiple modifications. The lower area of the planes serves mainly as a cargo space, carrying luggage and food supplies. It can contain food for up to 2,000 people when it is fully loaded, some of them stored in freezers. Meals are prepared in two kitchens, which are equipped to feed 100 people at a time.

The main passenger area is located on the second floor, and the communications equipment and cabin are located on the third floor.

In the office area, the mythical Air Force One has access to photocopier services, printers, word processors, Broadband Internet, Mobile Networks, as well as telecommunications systems, including 85 telephones and 19 televisions. There are also secure and unsecured fax services, and data networks. Most of the furniture on board has been manufactured by hand by professional carpenters.

White phones are for normal communications while black phones are for confidential communications. It also has a real-time conference room, internet, satellite TV and radio communications. All communications, including those of the crew to other crew members on the plane, pass through a command center that verifies that there is no interference, and from it they communicate with the ground to report the arrival of the plane.

All models of the presidential plane function as a military command center in the event of an incident such as a nuclear attack. Operational modifications include the possibility of in-flight resupply and an anti-aircraft missile system.

The electronics on board are connected with approximately 383 km of cable, twice as much as a regular 747. All cables are covered by a strong shield that protects them from electromagnetic pulse attacks in the event of a nuclear attack. Aircraft also have electronic countermeasures (ECMs) to interfere with enemy radars and flares to prevent missiles that look for heat sources. Many of the features of the Air Force One are considered classified information for security reasons.

The legendary Boeing 747 model has traveled the world under the name of Air Force One, moving presidents and leaders of the highest rank in recent decades. Since 1990, it has received modifications and updates in all its flight and defense systems, complying with the highest safety standards for the protection of heads of state.

With the arrival of the government of President Donald Trump, a complete modification of the aircraft was proposed opting for the most advanced model of the Boeing 747 fleet to its most recent version of the 747-800 completely modified and customized for presidential flights.

The new model of the presidential plane proposed by Boeing is the result of the requirements of the United States government based on more than 50 years of using these incredible flying strengths. "The flying oval office," as Boeing calls it, proposes not only a change in its exterior paint aesthetics, but also a series of modifications related to performance and operational safety.

The change of the mythical model was presented by President Donald Trump himself, who in his oval office presented the new design to the media around the world. Below is a comparison of the two models based on the official information of the Boeing company:

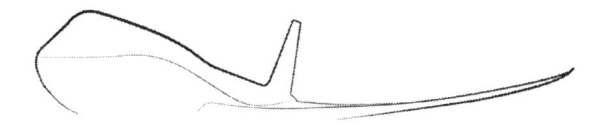

747-200/747-8 COMMERCIAL JET COMPARISON

CO_2 EMISSIONS

THE 747-8 EMITS 16 TONS LESS PER TRIP OVER THE 747-200
IT WOULD TAKE 13 ACRES OF AVERAGE U.S. FOREST TO SEQUESTER ANNUALLY

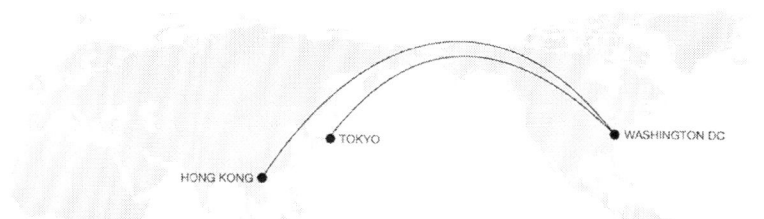

● TOKYO ● WASHINGTON DC
HONG KONG ●

6,735nmi RANGE **7,730nmi**

THE 747-8 COMMERCIAL JET CAN FLY YOU FROM WASHINGTON DC TO HONG KONG.
THAT'S 1,000 MILES FARTHER THAN THE 747-200 COMMERCIAL JET.

.84 Mach CRUISE SPEED **.855 Mach**

AT A CRUISE SPEED OF .855 MACH, THE 747-8 IS THE FASTEST COMMERCIAL JET IN THE WORLD

833,000lb MAXIMUM TAKEOFF WEIGHT **987,000lb**

A 154,000LB DIFFERENCE

195ft 8in   WINGSPAN   **224ft 5in**

THE DIFFERENCE BETWEEN THE 747-200 AND 747-8 IS 29 FT - ALMOST AS FAR AS THE WORLD RECORD LONG JUMP AT 29FT 4IN

231ft 10in   LENGTH   **250ft 2in**

AT 18 FEET 4 INCHES LONGER, THE 747-8 IS THE LONGEST COMMERCIAL JET IN THE WORLD

Undoubtedly, the new model of the United States presidential plane will make a huge difference from its predecessor. Although it will be difficult to know the new military equipment that the aircraft possesses, it is considered that it will far surpass its predecessor.

Aviation lovers who want to get to know the presidential plane in its entirety can do so at the Presidential Hangar of the National Air Force Museum of the United States at Wright-Patterson Air Base in Ohio, as well as at the Flight Museum in Seattle, Washington.

France presidential aircraft (Airbus)

The government of the French Republic uses an Airbus 330-220 as its flagship aircraft. Its original capacity of 324 seats has been transformed into a VIP plane with about sixty seats.

It has a bedroom and a presidential office, bathrooms, and a meeting room. According to the French Ministry of Defense, it has all modern, safe and reliable means of security and communication.

Both the meeting room and the rest sector have state-of-the-art communications systems, digital services, and rest area.

The French Air Force is the body in charge of operating the aircraft of the president of France, which is called "Cotam Unité" when the president travels on it (similar to the nickname Air Force One).

The latest model of the French presidential plane incorporates a missile detection and evasion system that makes it an extremely safe aircraft for transporting leaders over overflight regions that may be threatened by conflicts.

The magnificent French presidential plane is one of the main symbols of the Airbus company offering a long-range model, specially customized for the transfer of the president and equipped with a security system similar to the United States presidential plane. Both Air Force One and Cotam Unité are the emblems of the leading companies in the market (Boeing and Airbus).

Mexico presidential aircraft (Boeing)

Since 1947 with the government of President Miguel Valdés, Mexico has incorporated different models of presidential planes over the decades. The latest and most eccentric addition as a presidential plane was hand in hand with Boeing with its new B787-800 model. A state-of-the-art presidential aircraft equipped with the highest technology but which had a short life at the service of the head of state. It only had 214 operations. It went into operation in February 2016 and was used for two years and 10 months. At the end of 2018, President López Obrador decided to sell the entire presidential aviation fleet and travel in commercial aircraft.

The Boeing 787-8 had different luxury equipment such as a meeting room fully equipped with the latest technology, a section of traditional seats similar to the first class of a commercial plane, a presidential bedroom, a marble-clad bathroom, and the interior wore ornaments with official seals of the Mexican government.

The abundant amenities made this Boeing 787 an executive model lacking the military defense systems that the two previous models had, the French presidential plane and the United States presidential plane.

Germany presidential aircraft (Airbus)

Black, red, and gold melt into white in a real $238 million German beauty. The Airbus 340, also known as the Konrad Adenauer after the famous German statesman, witnessed good deeds as it was used to help evacuate Libyan citizens in distress in 2011. Power and precision are the main features of this plane that can fly a maximum of 15,556.8 kilometers without stopping. It has a capacity for 143 passengers who can enjoy rooms, a VIP cabin, and first-class service.

At the beginning of 2020, the German Ministry of Defense decided to replace the presidential aircraft fleet of Airbus 340 with the latest engineering wonder of this same manufacturer, the Airbus 350.

The new A350 models have greater comfort in all their environments than their predecessor, making a clear difference in technology and modernization of the ambience.

It has an electronic warfare system or EW (electronic warfare) for missile defense, a secure communications system through encrypted frequencies, and a reconfiguration of its interior by modifying a large meeting room for military operations.

With this new model of presidential aircraft, Airbus has managed to exceed expectations and combine all the characteristics of an aircraft equipped with eccentricities and luxurious comforts with a state-of-the-art military aircraft.

Japan presidential aircraft (Boeing)

Japan is another country that has always chosen Boeing aircraft. Since 1991, the Japanese government has operated two Boeing 747-400 aircraft carrying heads of government and members of the country's imperial family. They are set with 141 seats in special compartments, including a private room, meeting rooms, living room, and common area.

After almost three decades of operating in the service of the country, the Japanese government decided to replace the two presidential aircraft (B747-400) with an updated model with better performance and superior technology.

Continuing the tradition, the Japanese government again chose the Boeing company for the transportation of its leaders, but in this case, it opted for the 777-300 model acquiring two units. The planes have a VIP configuration; 106 seats are intended for the media and companions, it also has business seats, a lounge, and special spaces for His Highness and Prime Minister.

Similar to the model of the Mexican presidential plane, it is known that the Japanese presidential plane is oriented to a model more similar to a commercial executive plane and not to an aircraft with military performance. Of course, it is well known that some technical safety characteristics in these aircraft are not usually declared to the public to preserve safety.

Chapter 4

A320 vs B737

Introduction

The "trade war" for the domination of the skies has presented various battles throughout history. The aeronautical industry has witnessed countless models that have tried to conquer the skies over the decades, but only a few managed to transcend time and reach the present time yet struggling.

Both Boeing and Airbus have been the leading companies in the aeronautical market in recent decades. Each of these companies has put extremely successful aircraft on the market, which in some cases have had a certain useful life and in other cases continue to lead the aeronautical market to this day.

This chapter covers the duel between the two most flown aircraft in the world, both in the commercial aviation industry and in the private or executive industry. These are the B737 and A320 models in all their versions. Two aircraft of similar characteristics and performance that comprise a similar audience of short-range cabotage and international flights. The cost-benefit ratio of these two aircraft has made it possible to position their respective companies as leaders in suppliers of commercial aircraft in this range. Although the B737 is an aircraft with more years of experience than the A320, the latter has managed to adapt to the needs of the field and the constant evolution of its main competitor.

Below are all the models that have existed of these two wonders of aeronautical engineering and then make a comparison and offer the reader the possibility of drawing their own conclusions about which one he thinks is the aircraft that best suits the market.

Airbus A320 models

The Airbus A320 marked the introduction of the European manufacturer in the profitable sector of single-aisle aircraft with more than 100 passengers. After the A300, the A310 and the A300-600, the A320 was the fourth type of aircraft developed by Airbus, which entered service in 1988. The creation of this aircraft marked a milestone in aviation as it was the first aircraft to use fly-by-wire and joysticks instead of the classic control levers. To pilot it, only two people are needed (that is, you do not need a flight engineer), and its maintenance and diagnostic systems are centralized, which allows mechanics to check the aircraft's systems from the cockpit.

One of the great achievements of this Airbus A320 was to generate a family of aircraft that share a common design, but that is a little smaller (A318 and A319) or larger (A321). A pilot who can pilot an airplane of this family can pilot them all with a small adaptation course.

The history of the A320 began in June 1981 when Airbus announced the launch of the program, because the marketing studies handled by the company at that time showed a strong demand for single-aisle aircraft, as a result of the fact that the fleets of the initial B727, B737 and DC-9 were going to be out of service by the end of that decade. The project was officially launched in March 1984 after receiving an order for 50 units from Air France.

The new A320 could carry 150 passengers 3,440 km away. Its A320-200 version would later incorporate a central fuel tank that would allow it to increase its capacity from 15,590 liters to 23,450 liters, thus making it possible to increase the range to 5280 km. The A320 also had an internal fuselage diameter of 3.7 m, above the 3.45 m of the B737, which increased the comfort of passengers at the cost of increasing their weight.

Over the years, the new A320 was gaining skies around the world, adding operators year after year. Orders from the factory were increasing and getting closer and closer to the market that had been exploited by its competitor, the B737. In the mid-1990s, the other members of the A320 family arrived and covered a larger and smaller passenger market without detracting from profitability. Currently, A320 Family models are operated around the world and lead the market.

The years were ongoing and companies were placing more and more orders for this aircraft. Due to the demand of the aeronautical industry in permanent updating, Airbus planned a great leap in the most successful range of aircraft it had ever had, proposing a relaunch of the famous A320 with features that would surpass the new offers offered by Boeing with its B737 models.

Thus, on December 1, 2010, Airbus officially launched a new generation of the A320 family called the A320neo (New Engine Option). This new version offered CFM International LEAP-1A or Pratt & Whitney PW1000G engines, improvements in the structure and the incorporation of sharklets, which allowed fuel savings of up to 15%. Various benefits that seduced numerous airlines in search of optimizing their resources.

Virgin America was going to be the planned launch customer of the A320NEO but it was switched to Qatar Airways for that honor, although it rejected its first delivery due to engine problems. Finally, it was Lufthansa who received the first A320NEO.

By the end of 2011, more than 20 airlines had already placed orders totaling 1,196 aircraft of the A320neo family, making it the fastest-selling commercial aircraft. By the end of December 2015, more than 4,000 aircraft of the A320 model had been delivered and, of more than 7,600 orders, more than 3,500 units had yet to be delivered. The A320 family is classified as the fastest-selling family of commercial jet aircraft in the world.

Boeing B737 models

The history of this wonderful aircraft dates back to long before the outset of the A320. No other commercial aircraft has been as successful financially as the Boeing 737. According to statistics, a 737 takes off somewhere in the world every five seconds and there are 1,250 in the sky at any time. Despite its great success, the 737 program was almost canceled at the beginning due to lack of sales, until the United States air force ordered 19 models, giving Boeing an opportunity to continue with the program.

But to become a great success, it had to go through its humble beginnings. The Boeing 737 entered service in the late

1960s. It was conceived to be an aircraft that could fly farther and carry more passengers (up to 100) than the current Boeing 727. At that time, Boeing had a lot of competition in the market such as the BAC-111, DC-9 and Fokker F28 models and was desperate to maintain its market share. To this end, they accelerated the $150 million project using up to 60% of the same components of the 727 program. The 737 was quite unique because it had the engines under its wings to better facilitate maintenance and allow the hull to be lighter. This led to six additional seats inside the cabin, increasing the total capacity. We have seen that this design persists in most modern jets today. Lufthansa became the launch customer of the aircraft, and United soon followed it with slight modifications to create the first variant: the 737-200.

Although this first generation of aircraft did not bring great achievements to Boeing, it was from the second generation of aircraft launched with the B737-300 model that the company began to lead the market. Since then, the B737 fleet has not ceased to amaze the world. The pilots have enjoyed the constant technological advances in the cockpits with each new model that the company has put on the market. The evolution of the cockpit was remarkable, from 737-200 to 737-800.

Boeing continued with the manufacture of its flagship model, but already in the 21st century the challenge was greater. Airbus was gaining the market year after year, so Boeing needed to constantly update its version of the B737 and would think about relaunching the aircraft to the market. This is how the idea of the MAX version of the B737 fleet was born. Already with a completely competitive market, the company proved to be an industry giant by managing to deliver its 10,000th B737. The honor of receiving this aircraft was the Southwest airline, which received a B737 MAX8.

The B737MAX family arrived with version 7, but it was version 8 that had the privilege of going on the market with a leap to fame. The honor of receiving the first member of this family was given to the Malindo Air (Malaysia) with a B737 MAX 8.

Since its first flights, the 737 has captivated the public and has four different generations that include 13 models, from the mythical B737-100 to the incomparable B737-MAX-10.

	Variant	Passengers	Range
First Generation	737-100	118	1,540 nm
	737-200	130	2,600 nm
Second Generation	737-300	140	2,255 nm
	737-400	168	2,060 nm
	737-500	132	2,375 nm
Third Generation	737-600	130	3,235 nm
	737-700	140	3,010 nm
	737-800	175	2,935 nm
	737-900	215	2,950 nm
Fourth Generation	737 MAX 7	153	3,850 nm
	737 MAX 8	178	3,550 nm
	737 MAX 9	193	3,550 nm
	737 MAX 10	204	3,300 nm

Already presented both flagship aircraft of the two manufacturers (Airbus and Boeing), below is a comparison of the two most recent models of these aircraft.

Titans fight

In order to present the characteristics of these two magnificent aircraft, we will counter the two versions of each model with similar characteristics in this duel. On the one hand, an A320 NEO and on the other hand a B737-MAX 8.

	A320 NEO	B737 MAX 8
Passengers	194	200
Autonomy	3400 NM	3550 NM
Longitude	37.57 M	39.50 M
Wingspsan	35.80 M	35.90 M

The cockpit

The cockpit design of these two large aircraft is based on the concept of "Glass Cockpit". A completely digital concept where all flight information is offered on screens with the highest resolution and informative detail. Both aircraft in their most equipped models have the HUD (head up display) system that allows the pilot to keep his eyes at the front while still observing the information of the flight instruments. A state-of-the-art system that has been implemented in civil aviation, since this flight system has always been used in fighter planes where the pilot must keep an eye on the front at all times and not neglect the information of the flight instruments. Both cockpit designs maintain the profile of the cockpits in previous models.

Airbus continues to operate flight controls with the sidestick system and Boeing continues to use the control lever system.

In the main panel of the cabin, both aircraft offer a digital information system, both flight and aircraft systems. In the case of Airbus, the panel consists of 6 screens, two for each pilot (flight and navigation information) and two central screens related to the aircraft's systems. On its part, the Boeing panel consists of 4 screens, two for each pilot which include all the information (flight information, navigation and aircraft systems).

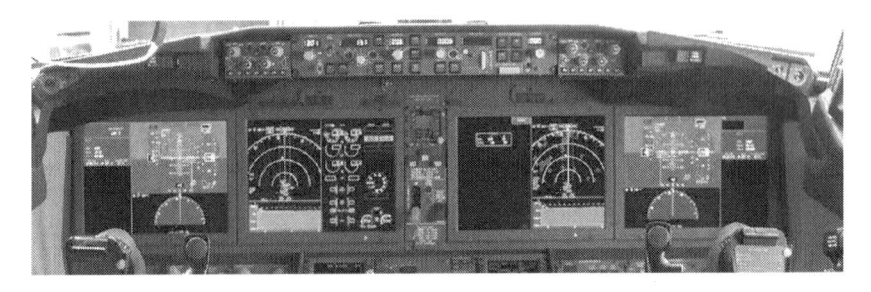

The top panel known as the "Overhead Panel" maintains the traditional style of the previous models. A fully equipped section in both cases, which gives the pilot the possibility to manipulate all the systems of the aircraft. In the case of Airbus, it maintains the panel style where the buttons and not the knobs dominate. On the contrary, both options are offered in the Boeing panel mixing buttons, knobs, and even similar indicators.

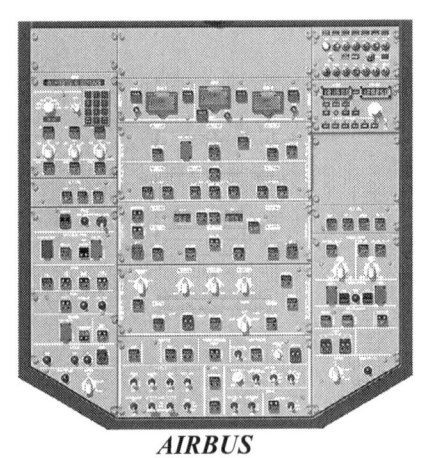

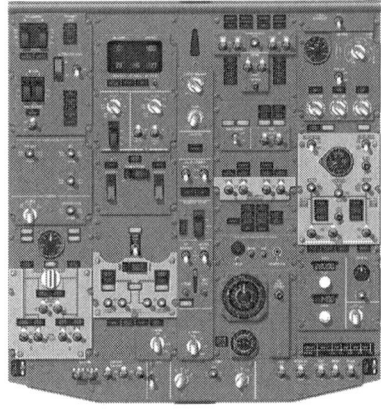

AIRBUS   *BOEING*

It is in the acceleration panel known as the "Pedestal Panel", which is where the great differences in the design appear. As for the equipment in this section, in both cases the panels offer duplicate

FMS system control, acceleration controls, flaps, spoilers, reversers, communications system, engine ignition control, TCAS system control and additional system controls.

The main technical difference is presented by the Boeing panel, which incorporates into this section, the fire extinguishing system of both engines and APU, a system that Airbus has in the overhead panel.

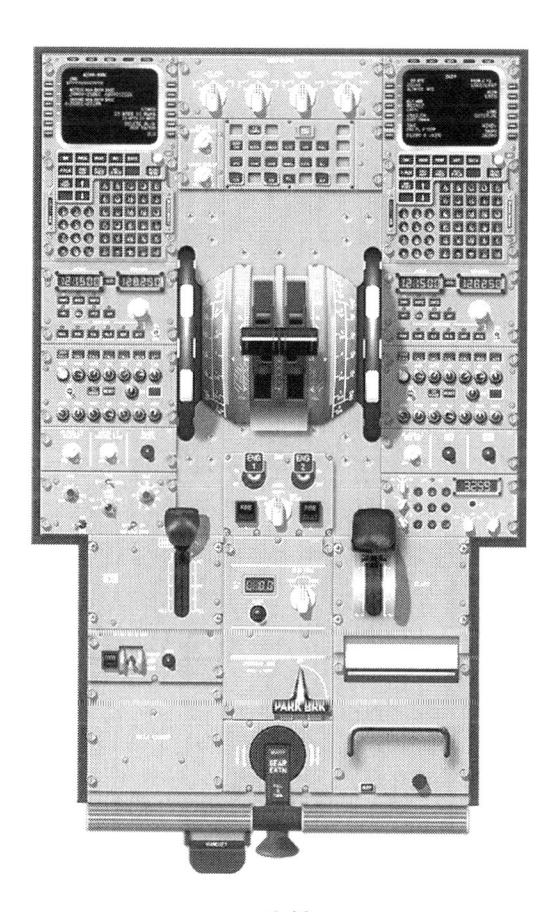

The obvious difference in design in each of these panels offers different advantages and disadvantages. On the other hand, the Airbus panel is a smaller integrative design that facilitates the manipulation of systems. On the other hand, the Boeing model offers more operational options by adding the fire extinguishing system but increasing its length, which reduces the space inside the cockpit.

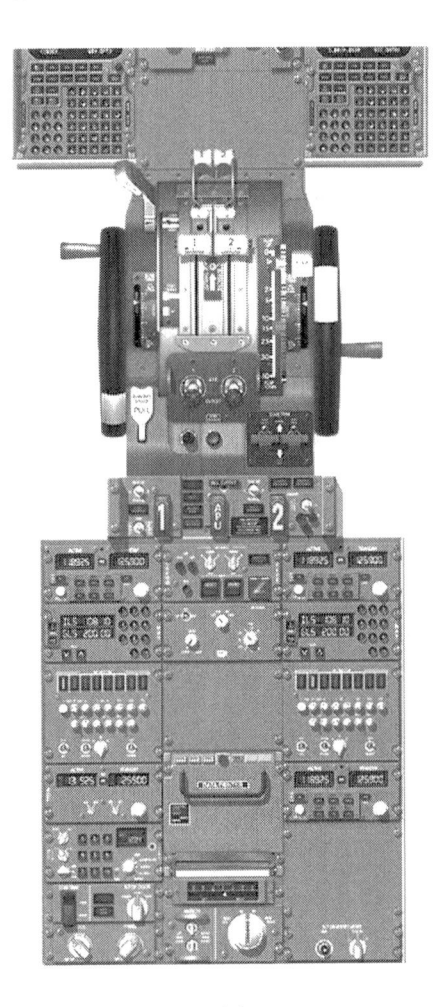

Another of the great differences offered by these two cabins is the incorporation of the HUD (head up display) system. The Airbus cockpit model offers the HUD system in duplicate, one for each pilot, while the Boeing model offers a single HUD equipment installed on the captain's side.

Passenger cabin

While this aircraft cabin is the section with the most possibilities of configuration for each operator, in both cases these two aircraft offer rows of three seats divided by a comfortable central corridor. With a personalized lighting system, both cabins offer the highest technology in design for passenger comfort.

AIRBUS

BOEING

Statistical data: The battle of these two grand of the industry in a period of time.

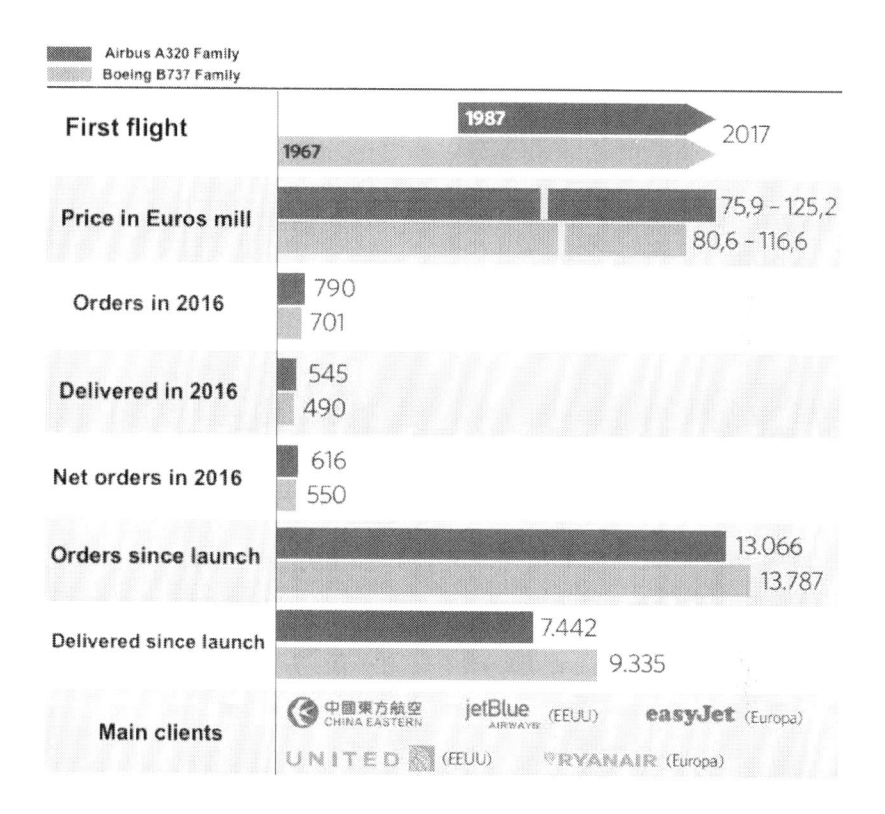

	Airbus A320 Family	Boeing B737 Family
First flight	1987	1967 – 2017
Price in Euros mill	75,9 – 125,2	80,6 – 116,6
Orders in 2016	790	701
Delivered in 2016	545	490
Net orders in 2016	616	550
Orders since launch	13.066	13.787
Delivered since launch	7.442	9.335
Main clients	CHINA EASTERN, jetBlue (EEUU), easyJet (Europa)	UNITED (EEUU), RYANAIR (Europa)

Statistical and technical data: The duel has not only occurred in the statistics of deliveries and orders but also in the cost-benefit ratio of each model.

On the one hand, one of the most important factors when deciding which aircraft to buy for a company, the value of fuel consumption. In this field, Boeing offered a 20% reduction in fuel consumption per seat, while Airbus reached only 15% of this same value. Other comparative values are detailed below in order to notice the difference between models:

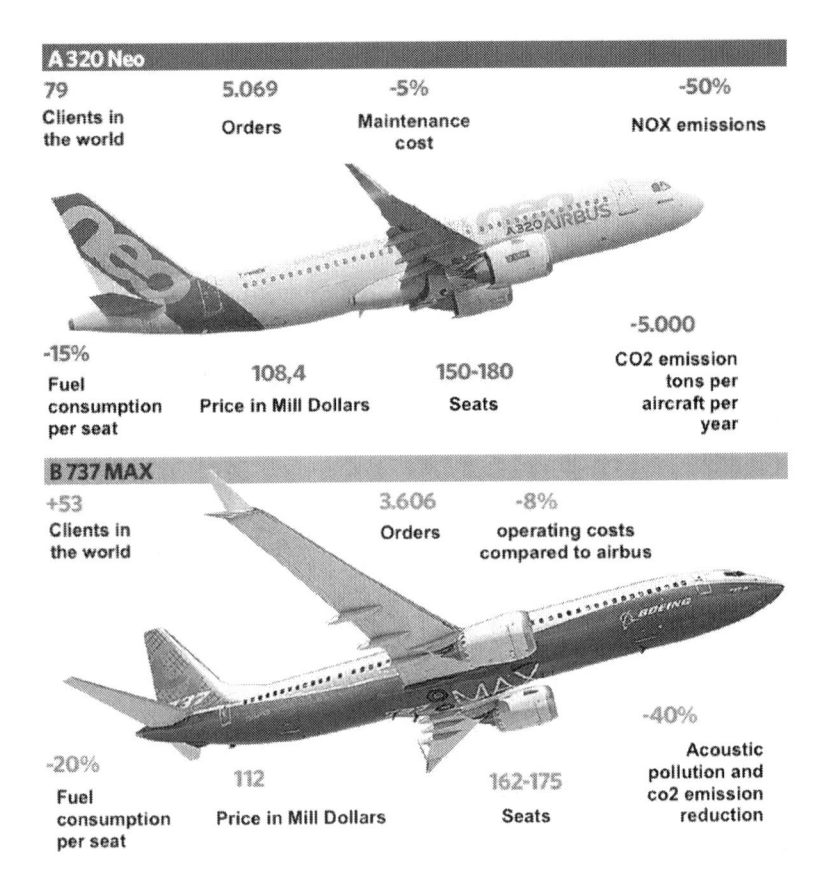

A 320 Neo

79 Clients in the world	5.069 Orders	-5% Maintenance cost	-50% NOX emissions

-15% Fuel consumption per seat	108,4 Price in Mill Dollars	150-180 Seats	-5.000 CO2 emission tons per aircraft per year

B 737 MAX

+53 Clients in the world	3.606 Orders	-8% operating costs compared to airbus	

-20% Fuel consumption per seat	112 Price in Mill Dollars	162-175 Seats	-40% Acoustic pollution and co2 emission reduction

148

Commercial data: Although these two majors of the industry have different benefits depending on the objectives of each company, when considering which of these two aircraft has been the most commercially successful in recent years, the information from the commercial statistics of both models must be analyzed.

Trade statistics 2010 2019

	A320neo		B737 Max	
	Orders	Delivered	Orders	Delivered
2010	30	-	-	-
2011	1.226	-	150	-
2012	478	-	908	-
2013	728	-	668	-
2014	1.009	-	861	-
2015	887	-	409	-
2016	711	68	530	-
2017	925	181	759	74
2018	562	386	694	226
2019	-25	52	106	20

Source: Airbus.com / Boeing.com

A320neo: Orders 6.501, Delivered 687
B737 Max: Orders 5.111, Delivered 350

Although it has been a competition with very close results, it was the Airbus fleet that led the trade statistics surpassing the Boeing fleet. But of course, a commercial statistical data is not enough to determine which of these two excellent aircraft is the best on the market. For this very difficult decision, various factors come into play depending on the operational objectives of each company.

As for the operational aeronautical criterion, they are two aircraft of excellent performance that can offer comforts and characteristics that other aircraft on the market do not offer, and undoubtedly meet all the operational requirements for a successful operation. Surely there are pilots who prefer to fly Airbus and others who prefer to fly Boeing, but it will be rare chance to find one that likes both models equally.

Chapter 5

Line of executive aircraft

Introduction

The diversity of executive aircraft stemmed from the need for large companies to transport their work teams. This industry took its first steps along with commercial aviation, where large companies and governments rented airline aircraft for private flights and requested the adaptation of their interior to offer an exclusive service to their passengers during the flight. This reconfiguration of a commercial aircraft for private use was based on maximizing spaces by removing seats in between and being able to offer a place with less passenger capacity but more suitable for meetings during the flight.

Quickly, the executive flight industry began to cover more market and came to the interest of the great millionaire tycoons who decided to hold of their resources by acquiring executive aircraft specially configured for them. After a constant growing demand, large aircraft factories began to design customized models from the factory to offer the customer a completely new aircraft designed specifically for him.

Thus, the market leaders, Boeing and Airbus, created a line of corporate aircraft in order to cover a market that demanded better aircraft and more luxurious compartments every day. This way, the business assembly lines known as BBJ "Boeing Business Jets" and ACJ "Airbus Corporate Jets" were created.

Taking as references their most efficient and best-selling models in their history, both companies began the manufacture of fully customized executive models with the highest detail in comfort, luxuries and performance of all kinds.

BOEING BUSINESS JETS

Boeing Business Jets brings the best of commercial aviation to the field of private air travel, offering customers a wide range of Boeing products that can be customized exclusively for the private, business or government sectors. The robust features of these aircraft also provide an excellent value proposition when they are equipped for the private market; offering a larger and more personalized space, unparalleled reliability and global support. Most of the time, customers want to have access to the same amenities in the air as on the floor, such as office, bedroom, shower, dining rooms, entertainment areas and more. Boeing Business Jets offers all these features with the highest detail in each section.

BBJ's executive aircraft family includes most of the models in the factory but with specific designs adapted to the needs of the market and with completely customized models.

Photographic sources: official website of Boeing and Greenpoint Technologies

BBJ 747-8

It is the Boeing giant at the service of corporate aviation. The latest model of the Boeing 747-800 adapted with infinite comforts offered in different possible configurations:

The BBJ 747 offers a capacity of up to 100 passengers with various comforts and luxuries in each of its spaces. The technical characteristics are similar to those of the commercial model. With exclusive details, BBJ offers various options for each of the aircraft's environments.

Reception or main room

For this first area of contact with customers, Boeing offers three different options capable of captivating all types of audiences. All three options offer different comforts and avant-garde designs. Luxury and comfort reign in each of them.

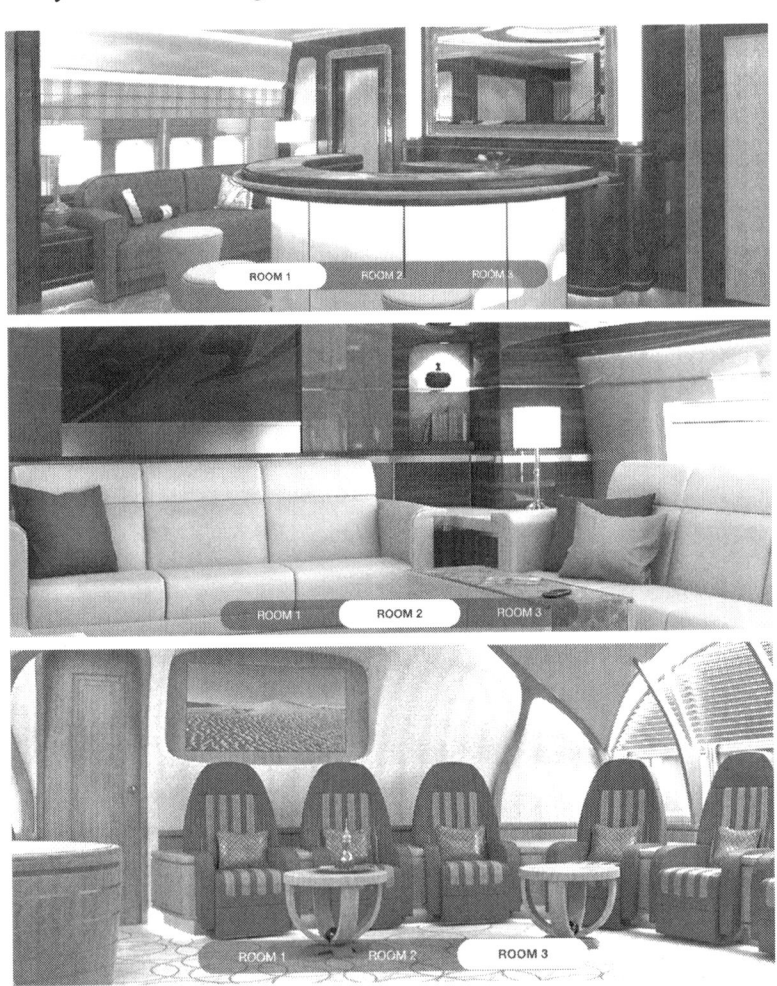

Photographic sources: official website of Boeing and Greenpoint Technologies

Office or private room

The concept of moving the company's office to the aircraft itself is reflected in these two options offered by Boeing for the design of a private office or room on your aircraft.

Photographic sources: official website of Boeing and Greenpoint Technologies

Central room

The central lounge offers the possibility of adapting to an elegant dinner among passengers, or becoming a spacious and comfortable meeting room. All the possibilities are designed for this room, from a formal meeting such as dinner between presidents or royalty members, to a corporate meeting between the members of the board.

Photographic sources: official website of Boeing and Greenpoint Technologies

Relax room

At the time of rest, this aircraft offers two possibilities to find a relaxation space where the occupants can relax and rest comfortably before returning to work.

Bedrooms

One of the most important areas of the aircraft is, without a doubt, the bedroom where the client can spend the flight sleeping comfortably and waking up in an environment exclusively designed for their comfort. For this space, the aircraft offers three options that adapt to all tastes and needs, it may be customized just like the rest of all the spaces of the plane.

Photographic sources: official website of Boeing and Greenpoint Technologies

Additional sections

An additional section in most models is the traditional seating section for the rest of the occupants of the aircraft but without losing exclusive details of comfort and luxury in its furniture.

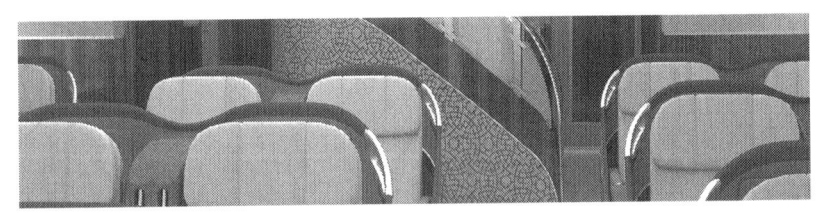

Photographic sources: official website of Boeing and Greenpoint Technologies

Another peculiarity of this magnificent work is the incorporation of an exclusive elevator to board the plane from the airport platform to the main reception room.

Photographic sources: official website of Boeing and Greenpoint Technologies

With an immensity of details of luxury and comfort, the BBJ 747-800 has become the most coveted executive model by an exclusive customer portfolio of the highest level. In addition to this diversity of possibilities in the configuration of each model, each client has the opportunity to customize each of these spaces to their own liking.

BBJ 787

Boeing's most advanced model and its most recent achievement turned into an executive aircraft with the highest technology in all its environments.

Central section

The central section of the aircraft offers an open and fully equipped space to accommodate its passengers in maximum comfort.

Photographic sources: official website of Boeing and Greenpoint Technologies

Living section

The Living section tries to bring the warmth of a home to the interior of the aircraft with different proposals equipped with the highest comfort and different designs for all tastes.

Photographic sources: official website of Boeing, Greenpoint Technologies, Edese Doret and Jet Aviation Design Studio

Meeting and dinner room

At the time of dinner there is a specific multifunction room that adapts as a meeting room and an excellent space to host an elegant and comfortable dinner.

Photographic sources: official website of Boeing and Kestrel Aviation

Bedrooms

Finally, the most important rest room of the aircraft, the bedroom and en suite bathroom that offer all the comforts and conveniences just like the rest of the rooms.

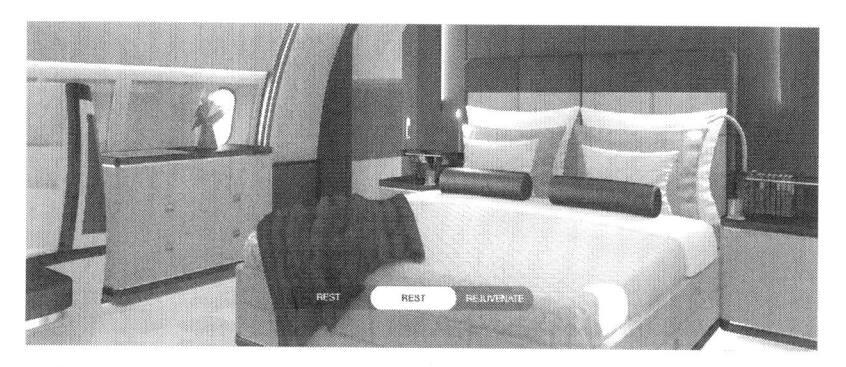

Photographic sources: official website of Boeing, Kestrel Aviation and Jet Aviation Design Studio

ACJ
Airbus Corporate Jets

Airbus' line of executive aircraft offers a wide variety of aircraft with the highest technology, comfort and luxury details that only Airbus can offer. Based on the success of its best-selling aircraft, the firm proposes small, medium and large executive aircraft with their ACJ-319-NEO, ACJ-320-NEO, ACJ-330-NEO and ACJ-350-XWB models.

The ACJ319neo, based on the product line of the A320 NEO family, with new engines and Sharklets, offers better range and greater comfort for passengers. With a range of up to 12,500 kilometers and a maximum operating ceiling of 41,000 feet and up to 15 hours of non-stop flight, it has become a small large giant of executive aviation. With the capacity to transport 8 passengers comfortably located, it offers a design full of luxuries and spaces with the highest level of comfort.

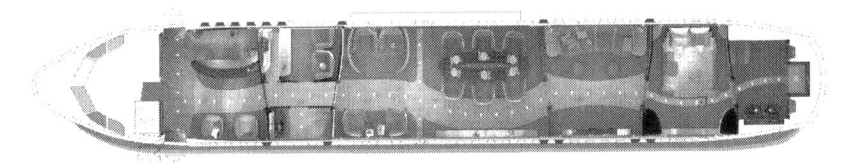

Descendant of the A320 Family fleet, this model offers a narrow fuselage executive aircraft, but combining all the features of a commercial aircraft and all the comfort of a private aircraft with the highest level of detail.

Photographic sources: official Airbus website

Identified as an Airbus flagship aircraft, the ACJ320neo model offers greater possibilities than its previous model. With a capacity for 25 passengers, it offers the possibility of opting for various interior configurations, from a business model to a family transfer model, but everything, absolutely everything, with exclusive details.

Family Setup

Faced with the challenge of offering customers the possibility of feeling "at home", a model was designed that includes various amenities, similar to home, bedrooms, rooms, recreation areas, all decorated with the exclusive level of detail of Airbus.

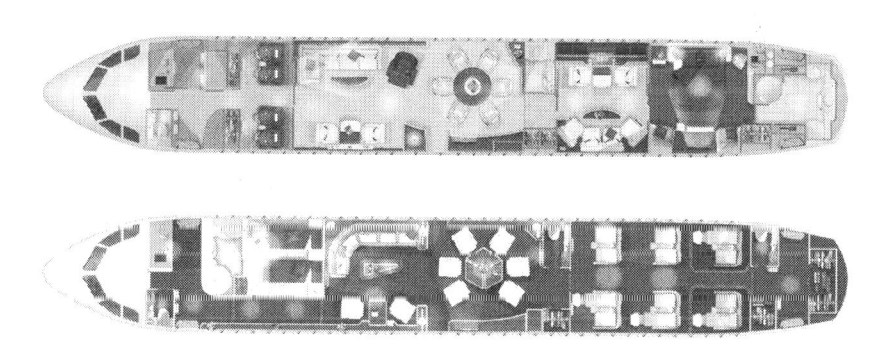

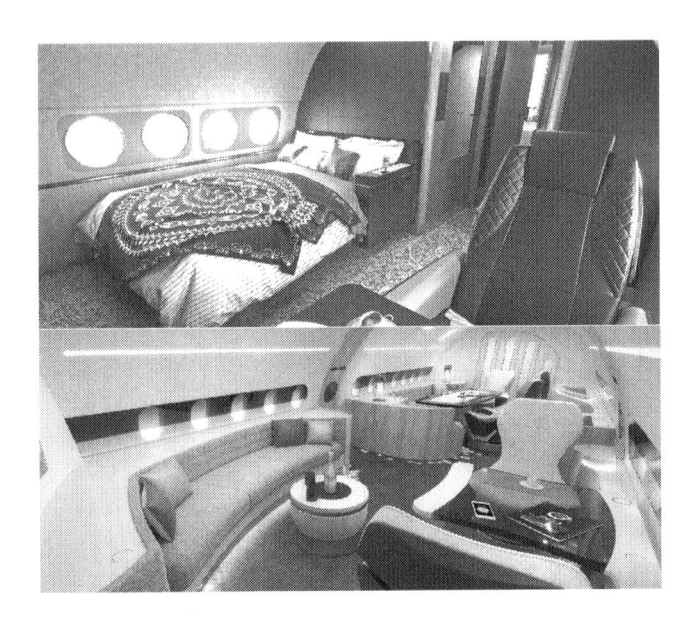

Photographic sources: official Airbus website

Corporate configuration

Finally, this version of executive aircraft offers a variation to all models and presents the possibility of a configuration for government operations, where each government seeks to meet its needs as a customer in executive transfers with state-of-the-art aircraft and the highest level of comfort for the journey of its leaders.

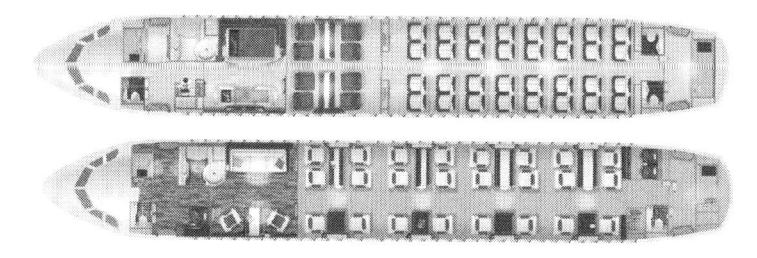

Photographic sources: official Airbus website

Government configuration

Finally, this version of executive aircraft offers a variation to all models and presents the possibility of a configuration for government operations, where each government seeks to meet its needs as a customer in executive transfers with state-of-the-art aircraft and the highest level of comfort for the travel of its leaders.

Photographic sources: official Airbus website

Both the ACJ319NEO model and the ACJ320NEO model are considered narrow fuselage aircraft with high performance but with limitations on passenger capacity. These models seek to reduce passenger capacity, maximizing comfort in all their spaces.

The ACJ330neo is presented as the executive version of wide and powerful fuselage. With capacity for 25 passengers, it can fly more than 19,000 km and 21 hours nonstop. This excellent engineering work by Airbus offers two different configurations, a superior comfort version and a corporate version designed exclusively for large companies and/or governments that wish to move a greater number of leaders.

Superior comfort settings

This eccentric model offers all the comforts that the client can imagine: conference room, equipped suites, lobby, office, VIP area, dinner room and an additional room for the entire staff of the journey.

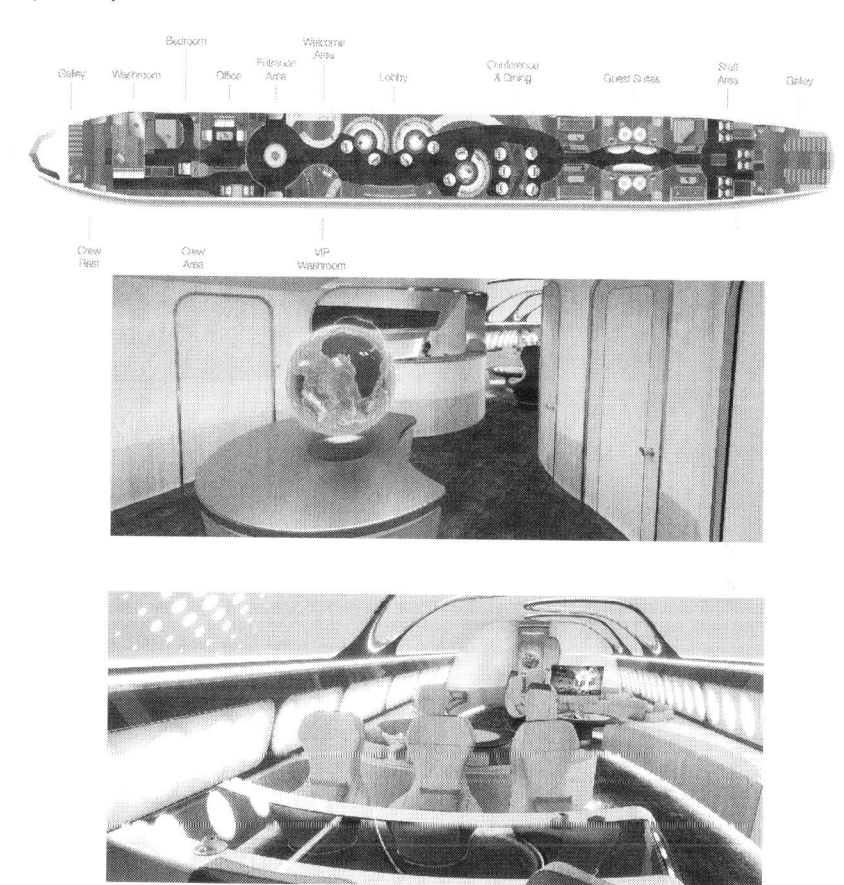

Corporate configuration

The corporate configuration of this aircraft is designed based on the travel planning of a complete staff. Companies with the need to transport their entire directory and the rest of the team look for this type of model to meet all their needs and be able to continue working in flight.

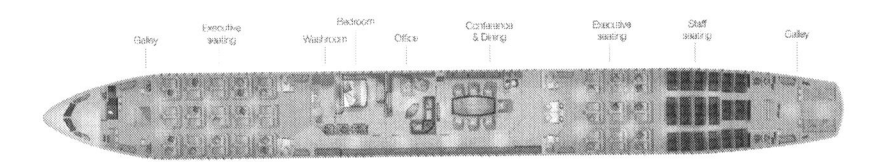

Fuentes fotográficas: sitio web oficial de Airbus

A complete multifunctional office equipped with the highest technology, a complete meeting room offers the possibility of continuing with all the tasks that a company's board performs every day. At the time of rest, this aircraft offers a fully equipped room.

Photographic sources: official Airbus website

Finally, continuing with the wide fuselage range, Airbus offers the market its most modern aircraft. The ACJ350-900XWB is made of 53% of composite materials, which allows a 25% reduction in fuel consumption compared to other models. A state-of-the-art aircraft that offers cabin designs for all tastes and needs. With capacity for 25 passengers, it can fly more than 20,000 km and 22 hours of non-stop flight. A true piece of engineering mixed with excellent artistic details inside.

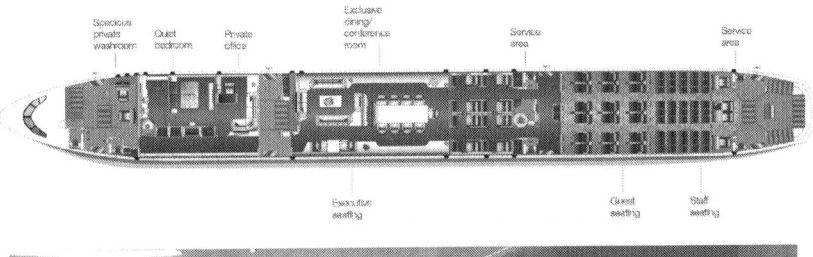

Photographic sources: official Airbus website

From the main room to the meeting room you can notice the excellent level of detail in its furniture, lighting and comfort of the entire environment in general.

Photographic sources: official Airbus website

The leisure sector is equipped with the highest technology and equipment to make flight a unique experience.

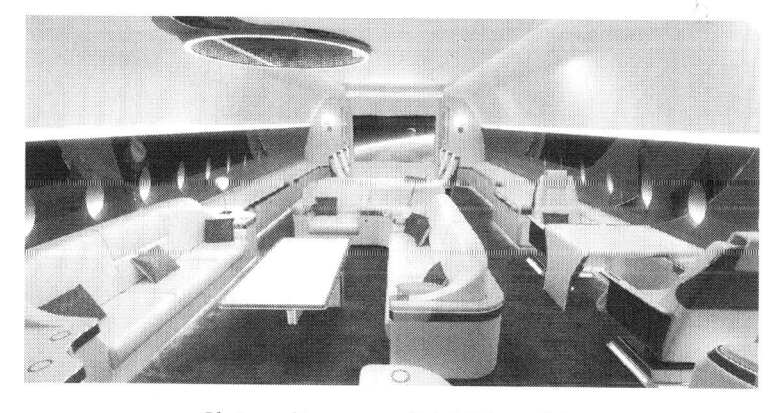

Photographic sources: official Airbus website

At the moment of rest and relaxation, the aircraft offers room designs with the highest detail and with all the necessary resources to achieve the best rest. Even, in some particular cases, it offers the possibility of adding a massage room maximizing customer service.

Photographic sources: official Airbus website

Chapter 6

Giants of the sky

Introduction

With the conquest of the skies and the commercial aviation industry already consummated, the companies sought to maximize the profitability of operations by all possible means. One of the values that used to be taken into account was the cost per passenger transported, a value that was obtained considering various variables such as: the operating cost of the aircraft, the number of passengers it can transport, fuel consumption, and other operational considerations.

Given the constant analysis of this value, the same result was always reached, it had to be possible to transport a greater number of passengers than any other aircraft on the market. For this difficult mission, as told in previous chapters, the head of operations of the company PanAm asked Boeing to take over this task and present it with a project that revolutionizes the market and guarantees the desired profitability. Challenging all the models known to date, Boeing presented an aircraft model that had two floors to accommodate a number of passengers never seen before. This project would not only maximize the profitability of airlines but would also give Boeing the prestige of manufacturing the largest passenger plane in the world, an achievement that it managed to sustain over the decades.

But it wouldn't all end with Boeing's incredible engineering work. Already in the new century it had a competitor who for several years had been proposing new and surpassing models that stole the market from the traditional aircraft of the American firm. It was

Airbus who decided to win competition from its rival Boeing in the conquest of the skies with the largest passenger plane in the world and presented an unimaginable model that challenged all previously known. Let's meet the B747 and the A380.

Boeing 747 models

From its first commercial flight back in January 1970 where it made the route from New York to London, until the end of the second decade of the 21st century, Boeing's magnificent engineering work has crossed the skies around the world with more than 1,550 units manufactured and sold. From commercial planes, large freighters, to the incredible presidential plane of the head of government of the United States.

Although the aircraft managed to surprise the world, it gave its first flights at the beginning of the oil crisis when the cost of fuel had become a problem for airlines. This led companies to pause all orders for this aircraft and Boeing to reconsider the business of this model. Looking for different alternatives, they found an opportunity in the

Japanese aeronautical market, where companies needed to transport as many passengers as possible but for very short sections.

This gave Boeing the opportunity to redesign its original model and modify a version with less fuel capacity, greater luggage load, more powerful engines and a maximum takeoff weight higher than the previous model. With all these features, the Boeing 747-200 was put on the market. This model managed to conquer the eyes of large airlines around the world, it was an aircraft that united continents and challenged the longest distances, but it would not be enough to meet the requirements of all airlines.

Airlines were pushing the 747-200 version to their limits and still needed more. It was from the Cathay Pacific airline that the idea of redesigning the already established model was considered. For this, Boeing proposed a long-range version with the possibility of configuration that offered a maximum capacity of 660 passengers and a range of more than 14,000 kilometers non-stop. Incredibly surprising values for the time.

Boeing continued to redesign and introduce new models to the market in an industry where a little more was demanded year after year. From the initial model, the Boeing 747-100, in all its versions (passengers, cargo and modified), through the 200, 300 and 400 models to the latest version manufactured by the company, the 747-800 in its different versions, Boeing has marked a milestone in the history of passenger air transport until the last years of production of this magnificent aircraft where it was threatened by advances in technology and the incredible engineering work of the competition, the A380.

To consecrate its success around the world and before its withdrawal from the production line, in June 2014, Boeing delivered its 747 number 1500. This honor was received by one of its great customers Lufthansa who at that time already had 76 B747s in its history.

A whole trajectory worth applauding, with millions of miles traveled and an infinity of passengers transported. Despite this, Boeing announced the end of its production line with the latest model developed, the B747-800. The inevitable advance of the industry led companies to look for more efficient aircraft at a lower cost. The new generation of aircraft has put an end to the legendary saga of large commercial aircraft.

Airbus 380 models

Since 1970, the giant that reigned in the skies was the Boeing 747 model. Over the decades, there was no competitor who could exceed the performance and capabilities of this aircraft. For its part, its main European competitor, Airbus, needed to continue offering competitive products in the market and year after year it launched cutting-edge models that challenged traditional aircraft in the industry, but there was still a challenge that Airbus could not overcome, the construction of the largest passenger plane in the world.

After several projects proposed by Airbus engineers, they found the right model that would try to break the record that the magnificent Boeing 747 had until then. Thus, at the beginning of 2005, Airbus made the official presentation of what would be the largest passenger plane ever built, the incredible A380. An extremely immense aircraft with two complete floors that occupied the total fuselage and that could accommodate 853 passengers in its maximum capacity, almost 200 passengers more than the maximum capacity of its direct competitor the B747.

This new giant of the skies quickly gained fame and prestige and was coveted by large airlines around the world who saw this work of aeronautical engineering as an opportunity to maximize the performance of cargo and passenger flights with a considerable reduction in costs.

The constant demands of the industry led Airbus to a constant redesign of the aircraft that has six models:

A380-700: With the official launch of the single model, airbus looked for a smaller alternative and created a version with lower passenger capacity to cover a lower market.

A380-800: This was the flagship model of this aircraft. It offered a higher capacity in takeoff weight, which allowed greater capacity for passengers and cargo. The first interested parties were British Airways and Emirates.

A380-900: With the launch of the incredible Boeing 747-800, Airbus needed to compete in an extremely demanding market and created the 900 model of this aircraft. A model that would be a little longer than the previous one and would accommodate up to almost 900 passengers in its economic configuration. Its change in length made this model the longest aircraft in the world. Although due to the resounding success of the 800 version, Airbus decided to postpone the production line of the 900 model since its main customers found the previous model more attractive.

A380 NEO: In the face of the revolution of the new factory aircraft with engine upgrades, Airbus developed the NEO model with a resounding change in the power plant of the A380.

A380-800 Cargo: As expected, Airbus had to take advantage of the incredible capacity of the interior of this aircraft to propose a cargo version and that is how it developed the 800 cargo model that would become the second largest cargo aircraft in the world preceded by the incredible Russian Antonov.

A380 PLUS: Due to constant competition from Boeing and motivated by technological advances and demands of the aeronautical industry, it was in 2017 at the "Paris Air Show", where Airbus presented its latest model of this aircraft, the A380 PLUS.

A model full of improvements, from a redesign of the passenger cabin that allowed it to place up to 11 passengers in a single row of seats, to endless aesthetic improvements in its interior. One of the big changes compared to the previous models was the redesign of the Winglets and an increase in the maximum takeoff weight. All these modifications led to a reduction in the cost per passenger transported from the aircraft by 13%.

Giants fight

A real competition of giants. The two largest passenger aircraft in the world with similar characteristics and manufactured by the two most successful companies on the market. The following are the main features of these two giants, the A380 and the B747.

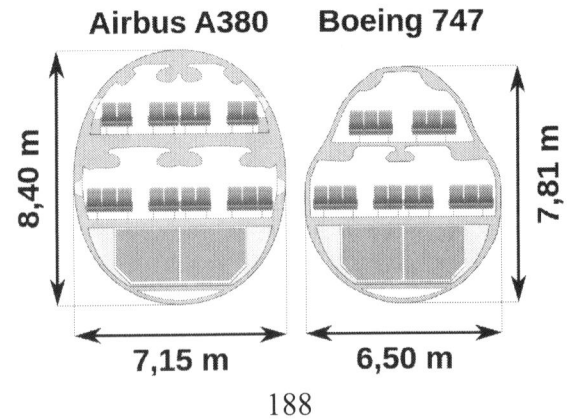

Airbus A380 8,40 m × 7,15 m

Boeing 747 7,81 m × 6,50 m

The cockpit

As expected in these two very advanced models, the cockpit is the result of the mixture of state-of-the-art technology and ergonomic design for pilots. Each of these manufacturers maintains the design format of its entire aircraft line. Airbus with the concept of a fully digital and more obstacle-free cabin, while Boeing a traditional cabin with different mechanical operation options.

In both aircraft, the concept of operational control of the aircraft is also maintained. On the one hand, Boeing maintains the traditional control controls, and on the other hand, Airbus maintains its sidestick model characteristic of its entire fleet.

The design of the bottom panel maintains a traditional format for each manufacturer. On the one hand, the Airbus panel offers acceleration quadrant, operation of systems such as flaps, spoilers, TCAS, communications, engine ignition, FMS and more. On the other hand, the design of the Boeing panel offers similar features to that of Airbus but in a more traditional format, just like the rest of its fleet.

In both cases, an additional screen of aircraft systems and the possibility of managing them by both pilots are added. The following are the two panels:

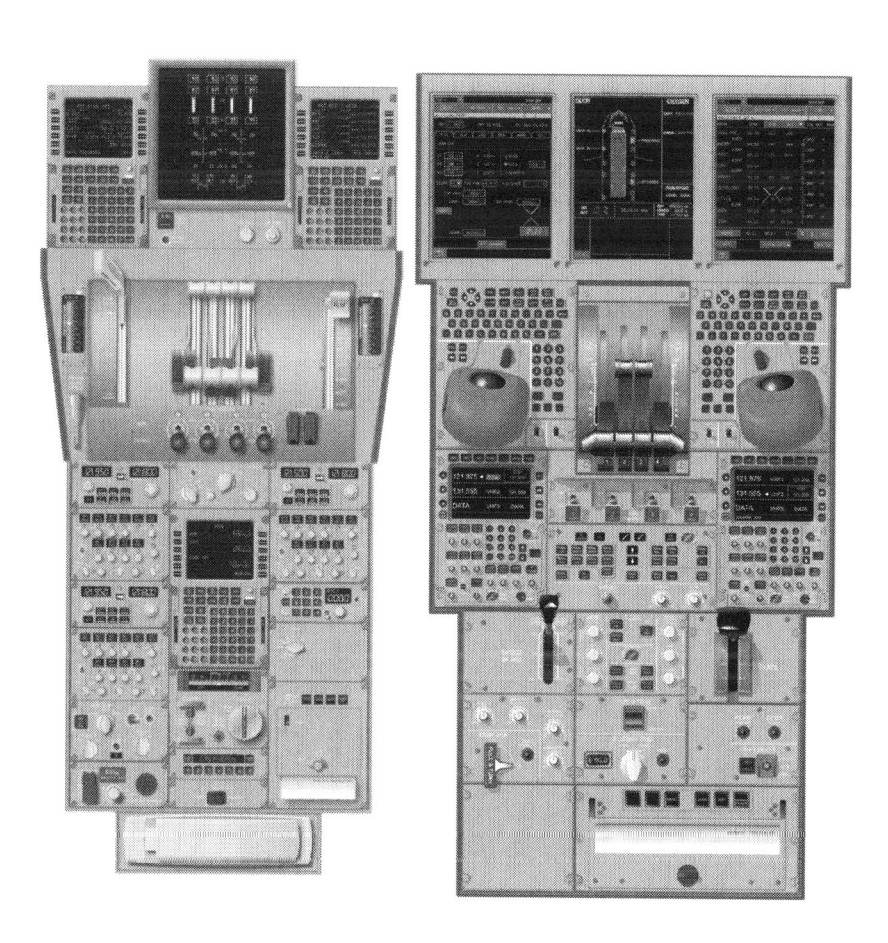

Passenger cabin

This section of the aircraft is one of the most versatile offered by manufacturers. Each operator can choose a certain cabin configuration and opt for different capacities, designs, luxuries, and other eccentricities that they want to provide to their passengers in the flight experience.

In a traditional cabin configuration, both models have similar characteristics with rows of seats equipped with entertainment technology similar to the rest of the aircraft in their respective fleets. Passenger capacity is directly related to this configuration of seats and the space between them.

It is in the first-class section where these two large aircraft make the difference. This configuration also depends on the requirements of airlines in the transport of their customers. While it is a completely variable configuration, in most cases Boeing's first-class design offers extremely comfortable sections with luxuries and exclusive attention of the highest level, while Airbus offers a variety of first-class designs where they can include even fully equipped suites for a perfect rest. The following is an example of Boeing in Lufthansa.

An example of excellent design and comforts in the first class of this airline where it offers comfortable seats that are reclining and made a bed along with an entertainment system.

For its part, Airbus offers another type of service in the first class section where the operator can opt for a traditional first class section with the highest luxury of details and amenities, opt for a premium first class with room service and all the comforts of a hotel, or opt for both options. The following images correspond to the first class of the Qatar airline, where you can see a seating section with a first-class design and exclusive to its customers.

And for the most demanding public requiring superior service, there is the possibility of accessing a real luxury room inside the aircraft.

Although these two large aircraft have been chosen by the most prestigious airlines in the world, according to statistics, the Airbus model has been the most requested by commercial airlines. Both the Boeing 747 and the Airbus 380 in all their models have proven to possess sufficient qualities to call themselves the kings of the heavens, the largest passenger aircraft in the world.

Two emblematic aircraft that changed the way of travel forever, will retire, due to the enormous evolution of the aeronautical industry, where airlines seek to optimize costs, not only for the passenger transported but also for various maintenance and operation variables, variables that the new generation of aircraft manufactured with composite materials are ready to face successfully, as Airbus and Boeing have done since their outset.

Printed in Great Britain
by Amazon